T

genius
within

ISBN: 978-0-578-92585-1 (print)
ISBN: 978-0-578-92586-8 (ebook)

Library of Congress Control Number: 9780578925851

Ordering Information:
Special discounts are available on quantity purchases by corporations, associations, and others. For details, contact www.mikezeller.com

THE •
genius
within

YOUR NATURAL PATHWAY
TO IMPACT, FULFILLMENT, & WEALTH

MIKE ZELLER

credit + dedication

To Sonnet Oceanna and Seven Sinclair I will always encourage each of us to pursue our deepest areas of genius.

To all my clients, friends and family, I will encourage and invite you to discover your deepest genius and fulfillment. I believe we each have a beautiful and divine purpose.

And to you, my reader, may you step into your deepest purpose, your deepest gifting, and your deepest state of abundance as you step into your genius.

I believe in you.

contents

intro

TO KNOW THYSELF AND THE COSTS OF NOT

"To know thyself is the beginning of all wisdom."
—Socrates

Kristen had just taken a massive leap of faith. This mom of two young children (and breadwinner of the family) had been dealt blow after blow. Her husband, Scott, was in a job transition and had no income the month she signed up for my entry-level program. He worked in the nonprofit sector—not a high paying role. In addition, their home had just been hit with over $10,000 in repairs. Credit cards were maxed. They had borrowed money from their parents to make it through. I didn't know any of this.

I could tell she had a deep hunger for a major career change, but she was also afraid. She had lingering questions—Am I good enough? Am I crazy to risk the last available amount on my credit card? Will this work?—and more—as she parted with her credit card to invest in her future with my introductory coaching program. I didn't realize how stressed she was or what a difficult hand life had dealt her in the last 30 days. If I had known, I might have stopped her.

Kristen Boss and I didn't meet by accident. She was ready to call forth her genius. She was in her zone of excellence as a high-caliber hair stylist. But she felt she was called to lead and to speak to the hearts of women. She didn't know it at the time, but she has a real gift for helping dynamic women in the social/selling world grow their teams and their businesses (network marketing). She's a magnetic speaker and communicator and she's now impacting thousands of lives through her Social Selling Academy.

Kristen and I went deep into four important areas:

1. Rewriting your money story. This is the lid of limiting identity for many of us.

2. Finding your zone of genius: your natural pathway to wealth, fulfillment, and impact.

3. Finding and reaching your four percent client: the client you are uniquely positioned to serve and who is hungry, ready, and able to work with you.

4. Creating your irresistible offer. This makes it easy for your ideal customer or client to say yes.

Kristen needed all of these and more. She needed belief and faith and a road map in order to live her life's purpose. She courageously took massive action and did all the work I asked of her—and then some. Four months later, she retired from hairstyling. Ten months later, she retired her husband from the nonprofit world, bought dream cars for her husband and herself, and paid off a massive amount of debt, all the while increasing her gross income ten times during her first twelve months as a coach.

But I'm not here to talk about Kristen. I'm here to connect with you.

You aren't here by accident any more than Kristen was. God, the universe, the source—whatever you want to call it—has brought you to this moment to tap into your gifting, your genius, your hidden, unique talents, and your ability to make an impact in this world. It's not an accident that you are reading this.

I believe God endowed each human being with a unique zone of genius. I believe that discovering it is meant to be a journey; your zone of genius is not a destination you will one day arrive at nor will it necessarily give you clarity for the rest of your life.

But I also believe there's a foe that opposes your growth toward your zone of genius. I know this because I've faced that foe many times and it nearly defeated me. In fact, it won some battles, but it didn't win the war.

In October 2019, I was on a fateful Zoom meeting with four team members I loved working with: "I have to let you go," I told them. "I have to shut down the business immediately." There I was, shutting down my agency, letting go of the team I loved, the team I'd built. Most of them had been with me for at least three and a half years. Terrific people, great talent; we had a cohesion that was rare.

But the business model wasn't working. I had just taken a knockout blow in a streak of financial blows and I couldn't afford a team anymore. After an epic string of wins and successes, I had seemingly hit a cold streak of failure after failure over the course of several years. I was juggling lots of balls, but an outside force seemed to be snatching them away one by one until I had no balls left to juggle.

As a high-achiever type, I'd gone from having 55 employees and doing nearly $30 million per year in gross revenue, to zero employees, no real business, no clarity, and absolutely no momentum.

In the days after the Zoom call, I'd take a lonely walk to the Portland Brew coffeehouse every day with a copy of *Heart Talk* by Cleo Wade,[1] trying to learn how to love myself. (This is especially hard to do if you're a high-achiever with a trail of recent failures littering your path.)

I experienced the full thrust of the divine storm: that season of your soul where everything that once worked no longer works—where everything you hold dear is ripped away from you repeatedly until you're left with bloodied, empty hands.

In reflecting on it, I started putting together the pieces of why things had gone wrong after so many things had, at first, succeeded. Few people had the deep pool of high caliber relationships that I had, and few had built as many ventures—but few also had as many epic failures. I began my deep dive into clarifying my own zone of genius by looking at my history, which was abundant with clues.

Let's go back to June 2018. My wife and I celebrated what some of our friends described as the most incredible wedding they'd ever been to. We'd hosted nearly 70 friends and family members in several beautiful villas in Florence, Italy, for four days, enjoying the birthplace of the Renaissance, eating delicious fresh truffle pas-

---

1   Cleo Wade, *Heart Talk: Poetic Wisdom for a Better Life* (New York: Atria Books, 2018).

ta, exploring the brilliance of Leonardo da Vinci, and feasting on what I consider one of the most remarkable cities on Earth.

But behind the beauty and the celebratory nature of the moment, I was a wreck. My cash-cow business—my real estate team—had disintegrated 60 days prior to the wedding. I had a real estate flip gone bad that was about to cost me a loss of nearly $250K. And my marketing and branding agency was also disintegrating, leaving some frustrated clients—people I considered friends, which made it even more embarrassing. Add to that, my clothing line was also hanging on by a thread with a zero marketing budget since my cash-cow business was gone. There was no way I could make much headway. Yes, I had a mastermind mentoring group for entrepreneurs that was doing really well at the time, but it was still a toddler business.

So on a Sunday morning in June about three weeks after our wedding when we were still in Florence, my wife and I got into one of the many arguments we would have that week. But this time, in a moment of intensity, she unleashed her fierceness and pent-up frustration in a very loving way while sitting and talking on the floor, "Babe, you have to let go of doing all these things! What is it people want from you the most? Your mind? Your ideas? Your beliefs?"

I didn't want to hear that because it didn't agree with my vision of the future. Feeling like a failure, I stormed out of the Airbnb where we were staying and headed to a café for a few hours to re-center myself and think and journal.

But sitting there in that café, I began to get some clarity on how I could navigate through the mess I was in and get to the other side. A big piece of that came by digging much deeper into my zone of genius, understanding what is in my zone, and letting go of the things that aren't in it. One of my core challenges would be that the work I'd been doing and the story of how I envisioned my future playing out didn't match my zone of genius when I unpacked it further.

I realized I had to reposition and get out of branding and marketing altogether and step into being more of a brand-as-thought leader and mentor. In my heart, I knew that mentoring held my deepest path of purpose and impact, yet I couldn't completely buy into the idea and own it right away. I had so many internal conflicts, feelings of imposter syndrome, and loads of self-doubt.

Maybe you find yourself in a similar situation, knowing that you're called to a different path than the one you're on, but confronting an old story, limiting beliefs, or other challenges that hinder you from stepping more fully into your deepest calling. You're also likely to wonder as I did, "What am I really best at, and how do I get paid to do it?"

I actually began creating my zone of genius process back in 2016 when I realized the entrepreneurs I was mentoring were searching for greater clarity in their own purpose and their pathway for profitability. The process is now in its fourth significant iteration, and two years from now it will have evolved even further.

In this book, I am going to break down exactly how you can gain more clarity than you've ever had in your life in answering the big question, "What on Earth am I here for?" And the question that follows it, "How do I make a great living doing it?"

Stick with me through this process and I promise you will gain a clear understanding of who you are, what you're a badass at, and what your natural pathway to wealth, fulfillment, and impact really is.

I must warn you, there is something sinister that stands in the way of your pursuing this path. That something wants you to stay comfortable, to linger in the arenas where you are merely good because your most magnetic, most powerful self is dangerously great.

Resistance is the name of that sinister foe. It will give everything it's got to throw you back down into your comfort zone. You may encounter people you're close to who question why on earth you would do anything different than what you're doing now. Judgment can swiftly follow. Business or career obstacles may press in. Doubts and imposter syndrome may scream in your head, taunting, "How can you be such a fool? You don't have what it takes! Who are you to think you can do this? You're not smart enough, successful enough, young enough, old enough, wealthy enough—enough!"

> "Resistance's goal is not to wound or disable. Resistance aims to kill. Its target is the epicenter of our being: our genius, our soul, the unique and priceless gift we were put on Earth to give and that no one else has but us. Resistance means business. When we fight it, we are in a war to the death."
> —Steven Pressfield[2]

Resistance shows up in many forms, but particularly in the forms of temptation and distraction. The temptation to hide and pretend rests within each of our souls and insidiously thwarts us,

---

2   Steven Pressfield, *The War of Art: Break Through the Blocks and Win Your Inner Creative Battles* (Egremont, MA: Black Irish Entertainment, 2002), 15.

whispering in our ears to stay on the sidelines, to play small, or to get distracted. You can be tempted to play in your zone of excellence, the arena you are good at, where it's safe and predictable. You face this temptation just as I do.

Playing outside of your position can have enormous costs. Part of my zone of genius is catalyzing movement, alignment, and brand identities in entrepreneurial projects. Project management and ensuring completion of all the details are outside of my zone. But it's still my responsibility to ensure those things get done and that I bring on the right people to make sure that happens.

Well, I didn't do a good enough of job hiring and thinking through my multiple businesses, and when my cash-cow business—my real estate team—imploded less than 60 days before my wedding in 2018, everything snowballed.

I wasn't in my zone of genius and I experienced the pain of epic failure; I personally lost over $1 million between 2017 and January 2020. I know the stress, pain, and sorrow that mistakes of playing out of position can cause for entrepreneurs and leaders who have their necks on the line. I often played out of position during that time. I lived and led from a position that was not aligned with my zone of genius, my deepest self. I stepped out, away from my power.

Your truest self is your most powerful self.

Your truest self is your scariest self.

Your truest self is you when you walk into a room as your powerful, unashamed, and confident-yet-scared self. You know who you are and what you're made for. You know what you stand for and what you stand against.

You own yourself.

The pursuit of knowing oneself is also the pursuit of finding out how great one actually is. Many a person has run from their own greatness, allowing themselves to hide in the shadows.

Yet I don't believe that's what you were meant for: hiding in the shadows and playing in your zone of good when your zone of genius is just a few shifts away.

I believe each human being is endowed with a unique zone of genius. I believe discovering it is meant to be a journey, not a destination. You are uniquely gifted and your whole life shows you clues if you know what to look for and how to organize the clues. Journey with me through this process and you will be able to move forward with greater clarity, certainty, and confidence than you ever have in your life.

For your zone of genius to be pulled into the fullness of your potential, it will take something bigger than your own ego; working for the greater good. Making an impact beyond your own acclaim, and making a difference in a time of deep need are all ways you may be more fully pulled into your deepest potential.

Consider this: legendary men and women are made in times of great crisis. We don't think of peacetime presidents as great, but Abraham Lincoln and FDR, who led us through the Civil War and the Great Depression respectively, are considered heroic presidents.[3] Compare them to Rutherford B. Hayes, whose greatest accomplishment was instituting the annual White House Easter Egg Roll[4] or Millard Fillmore (did we really have a president named

---

3 Arthur M. Schlesinger, Jr., *War and the Constitution: Abraham Lincoln and Franklin D. Roosevelt* (Gettysburg, PA: Gettysburg College, 1988).

4 "Easter Egg Roll: President Hayes Saves the Day," White House History, accessed April 19, 2021, https://www.whitehousehistory.org/easter-egg-roll-president-hayes.

Millard?) who passed the Compromise of 1850 that angered both the North and South and just delayed the Civil War.[5]

Having coached and mentored hundreds of high-achievers of all ages, colors, and sexes, I've noticed that those who consistently accomplish extraordinary success in an area of their life are the same people who sense their own exceptional alignment in that area. They are in exactly the right position.

Let's return to Kristen. She worked through the zone of genius process—the one I'm about to guide you through. Four months after going through the introductory program, she retired from her old career (six months ahead of schedule). Her monthly income had tripled (as of this writing she's increased her gross income ten-fold in 13 months). More importantly, Kristen is happier, more fulfilled, and more aligned than she's ever been. She's loving her work and getting great results for her clients. If you meet Kristen, you'll see she's one committed individual now that she's deeply aligned in a way that serves others at a high level.

Want the secret success formula? Read on.

I believe in you. I created this because I love seeing talented, amazing people like yourself find their unique pathway toward making a dent in the universe. I know there is a zone of genius for you that will provide deep impact, fulfillment, and the abundance you know you're meant for. Let's find it.

By the end of this book, if you've done the exercises completely, I promise you, you will have more clarity about who you are and

---

5   "Millard Filmore's brief time in the national spotlight," *Constitution Daily*, January 7, 2020, https://constitutioncenter.org/blog/millard-fillmore-misunderstood-or-a-disaster-as-president.

what you're meant to do. Will everything be spelled out for you on an exact roadmap? No, that's why you and I need a little faith and courage to make great strides forward.

By facing your fears and getting real with who you are and what you're meant to do, you will have conquered the toughest battle, the battle within. There is always another battle around the corner.

In my own journey, I played out of position for too long, I am resolved to work in my lane. I recognize that I need phenomenal operational partners for my ventures. I need people around me who are geniuses in the areas that I'm not, particularly in managing details and seeing projects to completion.

I've gained tremendous clarity in going through this process myself: I am more deeply aligned, my clients get better results, and I have more fun than ever. I can say with great confidence and certainty that I am one of the best in the country at helping high-achievers rewire their subconscious stories, recognize their zone of genius, and craft irresistible offers for their four percent client. I am also a badass at architecting the brand, the pathway, the key relationships, and the business identity for ventures I believe in. All of these things align with my desire to become America's top entrepreneur mentor—my zone of genius.

Be a master student of you. You will thank me, and so will your significant other, the people you work with, and—eventually—your bank account.

"To be a saint, means to be myself."
—Thomas Merton[6]

---

6   Thomas Merton, *New Seeds of Contemplation* (New Directions Publishing, 2007), 31.

self-acceptance not comparisonitis

"Be yourself; everyone else is already taken."
—Oscar Wilde

You become the labels you have accepted as true.

When I was in my epic season of transition and pain, I had moments of severe doubt, moments when I woke up and didn't want to talk to anyone, moments when I wanted to be the ostrich burying its head in the sand. But I didn't make a subconscious agreement with myself that I was a failure.

Instead of allowing my focus to go down a negative path, I interpreted my failures as temporary setbacks on the way to my success. In fact, since nearly every highly successful person has had significant growth pains and failures, I rationalized my failures were simply setups. I looked for evidence of this. I read books like *Failing*

Forward by John Maxwell.[7] I studied legendary business leaders like Rockefeller, Disney, Musk, Jobs, Ford, and others and found that their own journeys had massive setbacks, ultimately leading to tremendous breakthroughs. I listened to podcast discussions about this and so much more. I kept my mind and spirit fertilized with story after story of others who had defied the odds and rebounded from setbacks. As Jesus said, "Seek, and you will find." (Matthew 7:7)

My identity stayed strong and I kept wiring in and assigning a powerful meaning to my failures. You and I are meaning-making machines, we need to make sense of what is happening around us, which is why taking control of the meaning we attach to events, words, and more is one of the most vital things we can do—especially in difficult seasons.

Some of the superstars of our eras have decided on their labels, their identities. Beyoncé is Sasha Fierce when she steps on stage to entertain her fans. She owns that identity and label. Michael Jordan was the most clutch basketball player of his era[8] and is considered by many to be the GOAT.[9] Despite missing 26 game winners, he didn't focus on the missed shots.[10] Winston Churchill was the only British leader in his day to see Hitler for what he was

---

7   John C. Maxwell, *Failing Forward: Turning Mistakes into Stepping Stones for Success* (Nashville, TN: Thomas Nelson Publishers, 2007).

8   Kyle Daubs, "Ranking the 20 Most Clutch Players in NBA History…" Fadeaway World, April 16, 2021, https://fadeawayworld.net/2021/04/16/ranking-the-20-most-clutch-players-in-nba-history-michael-jordan-kobe-bryant-and-larry-bird-were-masters-late-in-games/.

9   "Michael Jordan vs. LeBron James: Everything you need to know about the NBA GOAT debate," ESPN, October 15, 2020, https://www.espn.com/nba/story/_/id/30108804/michael-jordan-vs-lebron-james-everything-need-know-nba-goat-debate.

10   "Without Failure, Jordan Would Be a False Idol," the *Chicago Tribune*, May 19, 1997.

and the only one with the conviction and backbone to confront those in power in Britain, despite his own political exile.[11]

How you see yourself determines your destiny. More specifically:

....

Your identity *precedes* your destiny.

....

When you have true acceptance around the good of who you are and know that mistakes are setups (not setbacks) in the long run, you're not in the comparison game. You're not trying to be a version of someone else (even though that person's story might inspire you). Your motive is to be an original version of you: your unique badass self. Embracing who you are, with your gifts, your warts, and your story ultimately sets you free to live with deeper alignment and to find your power.

You are uniquely different from me. Warren Buffett built his fortune in a vastly different way than Steve Jobs built his. Jeff Bezos leads differently than Jack Welch. Tom Brady is a very different quarterback than Patrick Mahomes. Lebron James is different from Michael Jordan who's different from Magic Johnson. Beyoncé is different from Madonna.

Yes, each of these megastars may borrow ideas, may find inspiration, and may deeply respect the others, but at the same time, they each crafted their own path.

For example, my buddy Nigel has built an impressive net worth, has paid for his dream home, and never has to work another day in his life if he doesn't want to. He's in his mid 30s and is incredibly risk-averse and disciplined with his money. I could allow myself to

---

11 "Leadership During WWII," Britannica, accessed April 19, 2021, https://www.britannica.com/biography/Winston-Churchill/Leadership-during-World-War-II.

be jealous of his peaceful existence—but I don't. I know my path involves far more risk, higher highs, and lower lows because of the traits of my unique abilities, my unique path for building wealth.

If you take the entrepreneurial profiling tool called the Wealth Dynamics Test,[12] it will show you pieces of your pathway toward building wealth. Nigel's pathway is more like Warren Buffett's: slow, steady, and deeply risk-averse. Mine is more like Steve Jobs's or Elon Musk's: high risk, high reward. I'm a "creator" on the Wealth Dynamics test. Buffett is an "accumulator." I'm good with that. I am wired differently and that's okay. Accepting our gifts and our uniqueness—not trying to be someone else—is part of the battle.

When you find yourself trapped in any semblance of jealousy or "comparisonitis," immediately interrupt it. Jealousy is a surefire way to block you from claiming your greatness. You can release comparisonitis by using any jealousy as fuel to find your own way.

Being swept up in comparisonitis, or jealousy, is also sometimes an indicator that you have real ability in that arena, but you have to be willing to step into it and get over your own imposter syndrome.

What if someone else is already doing what you want to do? Just because someone else is already there at a high level, doesn't mean you can't be there too. There are hundreds of thousands of people who write books every year. There may be hundreds or thousands of people who do what you want to do. That doesn't matter. There's someone who needs your unique spin, your unique way of showing up.

Choosing who you get inspired by is a critical and valuable decision. One of my favorite pathways to deeper self-discovery is

---

12   Wealth Dynamics, https://app.geniusu.com/store/products/21?a_aid=faefc12c

studying the greats who had the same wiring. The Wealth Dynamics Test is helpful with that as it sorts some of those greats into eight different profiles that you might identify with: "dealmaker," "trader," "star," "creator," "accumulator," "supporter," "lord," and "mechanic." For example, some of my fellow "creators" on the Wealth Dynamics profile are Steve Jobs, Walt Disney, Elon Musk, and Richard Branson. All of them are enormous risk-takers who are wired much differently than Warren Buffett, Oprah Winfrey, or Jack Welch. Their groups take risks too, but in a very different way than creators.

I've read the biographies, watched the documentaries, and extensively studied those who share the same Wealth Dynamics profile that I do. As I study the greats who are wired like me, I can see how they built their empire and avoided catastrophe or rebounded from failure. I become better equipped to manage myself—to lead myself—because I have studied myself and those who are wired like me. You can do the same.

The Wealth Dynamics Test is the only personality test that shows you your natural pathway for building wealth and hence, taking the test is one of the first things a client does when they join one of my programs. We'll dive deeper into Wealth Dynamics in later chapters.

"The great poets imitate and improve, whereas small ones steal and spoil."
—W. H. Davenport Adams[13]

---

13 ," W.H. Davenport Adams, "Imitators and Plagiarists," *The Gentlemen's Magazine* 272 (1892), 627–8.

the pursuit of greatness

FOUR STEPS TO ULTIMATE CLARITY ON YOUR GENIUS

"Genius is omniscience flowing into man. Genius is more than talent. Talent may merely be one faculty developed out of proportion to other faculties, but genius is the union of man and God in the acts of the soul. Great men are always greater than their deeds. They are in connection with a reserve of power that is without limit."
—Wallace D. Wattles[14]

Do you desire to be great?

I unequivocally do. I am also much less ashamed about that than I used to be.

The craving, the clamoring for greatness, the fulfillment of our highest potential is primal for many of us. Making progress is in-

---

14   Wallace D. Wattles, *The Science of Being Great* (Create Space Independent Publishing Platform, 2014; originally 1910), 4.

herent to desire and identity as a human being. You and I long to be more than creatures of circumstance. The longing to master our environment, ourselves, and our world is a core craving. But that remains a challenge for most of us—we've never been given a clear map, a clear plan.

Hence, the zone of genius.

This powerful process has the potential to massively increase the clarity of your pathway for becoming great. Here's the quick breakdown of the essence of the process (a more complete breakdown will follow in an upcoming chapter).

First, you'll identify your unique abilities through clues from the greatest assembly of personality tests you've ever had.

Second, you'll identify your unique life experiences as they indicate interests, talents, passions, and purpose.

Third, you'll identify key or pivotal relationships that are interesting to you and that bring you to life—the people who fuel your soul and your sense of purpose.

Fourth, your values and passions act as your final filter. They indicate where the fibers of your being sing and where they go silent. If what do you fits your gifts but feels misaligned on the soul level, your reservoir of inspiration will eventually run dry no matter how much grit you have or how many books by Navy Seals running on broken legs you've read.

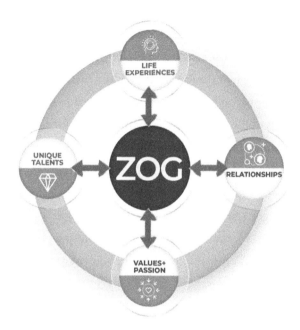

I know greatness is in you. And I know that when you have clarity on your greatness you can act more courageously and boldly, bringing your gift to the world.

Alongside the quest for greatness, inherently there's a quest for wisdom. Wisdom is the ability to perceive the best ends to aim for and the most effective means for reaching those ends.

When I was a kid, I thought becoming a professional baseball player was my trajectory. While I had the physical abilities and the drive, after playing during my freshman year of college, my soul longed for something more than baseball. A lot of things weren't working: I broke my nose two weeks before our season kicked off that year and promptly lost 25 pounds of chiseled muscle. (My nickname up until that point was "Beefcake," for a reason.) We had a new coach who was incredibly hard on us as a team and 50 percent of the team quit before year end. The season was miserable. Every aspect about it. I felt suffocated, we lost most of our games, and I realized my heart longed to explore other aspects of life.

I didn't know it at the time, but I desired mastery of the highest levels of me, beyond simply my own physical mastery. I desired the fullness of life and there was so much more for me to explore, so much more talent to cultivate.

Recently, I took my friend A. J. Mihrzad, a successful entrepreneur, coach, and podcaster, through the zone of genius process. When we got started, he was in a state of stagnation in his life and business. He wasn't feeling fulfilled or inspired even though his business was prosperous and his life was enjoyable. He needed some shifts in a bad way.

A. J. did the exercises I guided him through and we did a one-on-one phone call. By the end, he was blown away by the shifts he'd made and the clarity he'd gained. He felt he could own his power, his ability in new ways going forward. He got re-anchored to his confidence and conviction, which re-invigorated his momentum. Check out my podcast interview with A. J. on *The Online Supercoach* podcast. In A. J.'s words:

"You're doing this massive brain dump, gathering all this data about your dreams, your desires, and then making it super-concentrated…I really feel like everyone should do this whether you're just starting out or you're 10 or 20 years in. The greatest feeling everyone wants to know is, what is my purpose.

"With this specific exercise, I'm closer to my life's purpose than ever before…I feel a new sense of clarity, a sense of conviction and confidence, and my energy levels are so much higher as a result."

Becoming Great Now: Anchoring It in Your Subconscious

You do not become great by reading other people's great thoughts, shouting some mantras, and surrounding yourself with great people. You have to think and believe your own great thoughts and then act in great ways. It starts with how you think about yourself now.

Success author Wallace Wattles wrote: "Do not merely think you are going to become great; think you are great now."[15]

How does this play out? Instead of proclaiming to yourself, "I will be great one day! I will achieve X someday!" declare, "I am extraordinary today. I am a badass right now." Our words are our commands. Be careful with the words you think and use every day.

And after declaring, act greatly now. Do little things in a great way now. Give the moment, the people, the role, the task you're in right now your all; don't wait for an opportunity in the future to give it all you've got. Act as if you are the great man or woman you know yourself capable of becoming. You may not feel like you are that great, but you will work yourself into the new identity if you act it every day. If you never act as the powerful man or woman you know yourself to be, you'll never show up as that person.

> *"Whether you think you can or you can't, you're right."*
> —Henry Ford

One of the most powerful exercises you can do is a deep meditation and visualization exercise, imagining yourself to be moving, talking, thinking like the greatest version of yourself. Think of

15   Wattles, *The Science of Being Great*, 58.

it as stretching your mind to a new capacity so that it can hold onto more. When you stretch a rubber band, it expands what it can hold.

I have created what I have found to be one of the most powerful and unique visualization exercises; it can rewire your subconscious mind in a single session. I call it Claim Your Power. When I take clients through my Claim Your Power neurolinguistic programming (NLP) session, I've found that, in a matter of days, they can go from debilitating uncertainty about their next steps, to massive insight, confidence, and momentum.

Essentially, a Claim Your Power NLP session is a deep meditation process during which I guide you into a centered meditative state. Once in that state, we then identify a limiting belief, story, or identity that has been a part of you but that no longer serves you and that your body wants to release (typically your most powerful voice of self-sabotage). Through the meditation, you are then guided to understand the good intent of that old part of you, give it a name, and then thank it and release its control over you by asking it to give up the keys that are driving your life. Afterward we do a swish technique, an NLP process that shrinks the destructive memory's role in your life, replacing what you don't want with what you do want.

We search your subconscious to find a memory of a moment in time when you were your most powerful and magnetic self—the self that is you at your highest and best. You visualize and experience that memory again so that you see what you saw, hear what you heard, feel what you felt, touch what you touched, and you enjoy the memory. Then you name that part of you—whatever your body or your heart wants to name it—and ask that part of you to take an increasing role in leading your life.

And finally, we go to a time in the future when you will have accomplished what you wanted to accomplish or experienced what you wanted to experience. Your big lofty goal or dream that seems nearly impossible right now has been accomplished, and we experience that goal. Then we walk our way back along a timeline, experiencing each step all the way back to the present.

The beauty of this process is that you pre-experience each step toward reaching your goal by starting with the success of accomplishment. Your body and mind are already anchored to success as you blaze a path toward your goals through the neuro-forest of your mind. All you have to do is stay on the path.

I've never seen another process as effective as this one for creating rapid transformation and confidence. I've had clients leave behind 28 years of shame from family and friends and see their confidence soar. I've had clients leave behind deep emotional traumas that had cast a dark cloud over their life for many years.

When I took my friend Nick Cavuoto through the Claim Your Power session at a mastermind retreat, he was clearly uncertain about his future. He was in the process of closing down his multiple-seven-figure agency and he wanted to coach, but imposter syndrome and limiting beliefs were rearing their ugly heads. He knew he had gifts to offer and he wanted to pastor entrepreneurs, but he didn't know how he'd actually get there or if he had what it took. After working through the Claim Your Power process, Nick's mental and emotional fog lifted and he went from being in a state of paralysis to launching a new coaching venture with a $161,000 launch month in a matter of 14 days. He went from being stuck and uncertain to empowered and certain, which meant instead of acting tentatively he acted decisively.

Nick's breakthroughs came immediately after taking the Wealth Dynamics Test and realizing his category is "star," and then doing the Claim Your Power NLP session. Once he combined the two, he utilized his inherent marketing genius and gifts to absolutely smash a launch and he's been off to the races ever since.

One of the challenges to owning and claiming your genius is criticism, or, actually, the fear of criticism, which is often much greater than the real thing. Fears of what people might say about me, too, have often held me back from giving projects my all and going hard at whatever I'm creating. Criticism can lock you into the tightest handcuffs. So let's talk about criticism and facing those fears for a moment.

As you pursue maximizing your talents in your one and only life, some of the people you are closest to may criticize and question your ego, your character, and many things, like motivation (which feels the worst). People whose lives you've done a world of good for might suddenly find fault with you. You may find haters, internet trolls, and much more.

Receive the criticism as a twofold gift. First, if there is some truth, receive it and grow through it. Detach your ego from needing to be perfectly liked by everyone, as that is nothing more than a farce at best anyway.

People will judge you when you do something. People will judge you when you don't. You'll be judged either way. It's going to happen no matter what. People may be ungrateful, unkind, and critical of you. But remember the lives that will not be changed and the impact that will be missed if you play small. Switching your anchor and motivation from worrying about the critics to missing out on the people who desperately need you to show up as great as you are, will create the internal leverage you're seeking my friend.

"Doing great things will not make you great but becoming great will certainly lead you to the doing of great things."
—Wallace Wattles[16]

action item

Before we leave this topic, I want you to do a very specific thinking exercise to claim your greatness. Here's what I want you to do: Block out an hour, grab your favorite notebook, your favorite instrumental music playlist, and put your phone in airplane mode. Then, write out these questions, "What would it look like for me to step more fully into my greatness? What would I need to release to claim that greatness?" Then spend one hour writing four pages in that notebook to answer those questions. Afterward, you will have more clarity than you've ever had before.

Bonus: Do a Claim Your Power meditation session (free on my YouTube channel: youtube.com/theMikeZeller).

*The beauty of the Claim Your Power process in combination with your zone of genius is that it stretches your mind and your belief structure in both the subconscious and conscious realms.

"Everybody can be great, because everybody can serve."
—Martin Luther King, Jr.[17]

---

16   Wattles, *The Science of Being Great.*
17   Martin Luther King, Jr., "The Drum Major Instinct," sermon, 1968

to know thyself

YOUR UNIQUE TALENTS

"If you do not conquer self, you will be conquered by self."
—Napoleon Hill[18]

An inherent quest of all mankind since the beginning has been to understand ourselves in relation to the world we find ourselves in.

We ask ourselves:

"What on Earth am I here for?"

"Do I matter?"

"Am I truly exceptional at anything that is valuable or am I destined to be average?"

"Can I make a living doing what I love and what I'm truly good at?"

We crave significance and impact. We all want to matter, to leave a mark on this world. No matter your spiritual beliefs, you are reading this because, deep within, you want to matter more.

18   Napaoleon Hill, *Think and Grow Rich* (Sound Wisdom, 2019; originally 1937).

The ancient Greeks had the phrase, "Know Thyself" inscribed on the Temple of Apollo at Delphi.[19] It meant that a man must stand and live according to his nature.

The task for knowing yourself is far from easy, but it can be simple. That's what I'm going to help you with. Journey in and you'll find clues on how to journey back out again, effectively, happily, and lucratively.

In my own quest, having coached and mentored hundreds of entrepreneurs, leaders, and high-achievers of all types, I've learned that one of the fundamental quests is to know your purpose. Beyond that, you must find a way to fulfill that purpose in a way that is deeply aligned with your gifting and ensure you receive the proper compensation for the value you bring. We begin that by defining our zone.

In creating the zone of genius, I noticed that clues to each person's zone, their sweet spot, were all around but they were scattered and incohesive. No one had created what I considered an effective and organized structure to identify the zone of genius. Simply too much information was missing. People would take a personality test here or there, they'd have feedback from friends, coworkers, or family members, and, of course, they'd get clues from their work or life experiences. But no one had created a thoughtful, integrated, and rigorous structure.

Here it is. This is how we get to the heart of the process: the four key areas that offer the most clues about your genius. I break them down one by one: unique talents, key relationships, unique life experiences, and finally, values and passions.

---

19 Pausanias; W.H.S. Jones trans., *Description of Greece, Volume I: Books 1–2* (Harvard University Press, 1918), 10.24.

UNIQUE TALENTS: Nearly everyone has done a personality test at one point or another, but most of my clients couldn't remember their results, much less their meaning or the clues they gave. They knew that they had gifts because they'd had some things work really well in life, but, on the whole, their clarity as to what worked and why it worked so well was vague at best. This was a problem I felt needed to be addressed because I saw firsthand what a deeper sense of clarity about one's gifts could bring to their life.

KEY RELATIONSHIPS: When I began guiding my clients to write about some of the valuable relationships they were surrounded with—the people they most enjoyed being around—clues started emerging. For myself, I noticed that I found myself surrounded by highly accomplished entrepreneurs, authors, and leaders: creators, dreamers, and visionaries who longed to make their mark on the world. My closest friends were thoughtful, driven entrepreneurs and creators who had something to say.

UNIQUE LIFE EXPERIENCES: What unique life experiences have you had that set you apart from others? When I first did an inventory of my unique life experiences, a few things jumped out. First, at that time I had started 16+ ventures and had earned income from 32 different sources. I had spent 1,447 hours with Tony Robbins. I had invested over $500,000 in my own personal post–graduate school development by listening to some of the brightest and best minds in the personal development and entrepreneur space. I had read over 1,000 books. I had started businesses in at least six different industries. I also saw that I especially enjoyed my e-commerce entrepreneur days despite losing a good deal of money on my first idea, a men's clothing line. And I noticed that I came alive when I was in deep-learning environments and swimming in a rich world of ideas.

VALUES AND YOUR PASSIONS: Most of the entrepreneurs and thought leaders I have in my circle had a vague semblance of understanding of what their personal values and passions are, but few had real clarity. Having worked through this understanding in myself, I realized certain values and passions act as a filter.

For example, one of my values is that I believe there is so much divine potential in each one of us to do good in the world. I am very passionate about human psychology and studying how to unlock people's creative, leadership, and entrepreneurial potential while also expanding their capacity to love and to do good in the world. Those things align nicely with my unique blend of talents for seeing the connectedness of different pieces, idea generation, and helping people become unstuck.

Personally, I have been obsessed with learning and growth since I was 19 and my mom sent me to a $99 two-day Peter Lowe Success Seminar. I knew then I was passionate about growth, about knowing myself, and about making the most of myself. I've spent tens of thousands of hours studying and becoming a Master NLP Practitioner through an intensive 18-day certification process to develop the ability to create rapid-change skills.

Having experienced the pain of epic failure and losing over $1 million personally between 2017 and the first quarter of 2020, I know the stress, pain, and sorrow that bad mistakes of playing out of position can cause for entrepreneurs and leaders who have their necks on the line. I experienced such a deep well of suffering during that time largely because I had used my genius and my gift to start businesses, but then I had to be CEO and COO of multiple ventures, neither of which are my genius. Losing that much money and going through such a stressful season with my wife, I wanted to help others avoid that sort of suffering and stress. Even writing this little bit about that season raises anxiety in my body.

The pain I experienced drove me to create a process to help entrepreneur clients minimize their own pain. Your mess becomes your message, right? As I mentored and coached successful and early-stage entrepreneurs in many different industries, I noticed they all yearned for greater clarity for what they were best at and where they could add the most value while fulfilling their purpose.

No one had created a comprehensive process to bring all the clues together. Sherlock Holmes couldn't solve the toughest case with only a handful of clues scattered about. Arguably, to know thyself is one of the toughest life quests one can undertake, but one of the most rewarding.

Famously, Benjamin Franklin, in his *Poor Richard's Almanac*, observed the tremendous challenge of knowing one's self, with: "There are three things extremely hard: steel, a diamond, and to know one's self."[20]

Guiding and mentoring top performers from around the world, I noticed that my clients who put the most intentionality, the most focus, the most self-awareness around finding their unique pathway seemed to have the best chances to:

Win in their career.

---

20   Benjamin Franklin, *Poor Richard's Almanac* (Rosenbach Museum & Library digitized version; originally 1750).

Win in their life.

They found fulfillment. They found purpose. They found alignment. They found prosperity.

Did challenges exist?

Were obstacles in the way?

Was it hard?

Did they have to face their fears?

Yes. Yes. Yes. And Yes.

Early on, I took one of my VIP clients, Rob, through this process. At the time, he was making a healthy seven figures a year in his chiropractor practice working a handful of hours per week, which ended up translating to nearly $2,000 per hour when we did the math. But he wasn't fulfilled. A part of him was dying because he knew he was made for more.

I had him dive deep into this process. At first he was frustrated when he saw that he'd have to take a bunch of personality tests. By the end of it though, he was raving about how powerful the experience was. He had far more clarity than he'd ever had on his next steps in building his business and his zone of genius, which raised his confidence and his resolve to step more deeply into purpose and passion.

Now he's sold his chiropractic practice and he and his wife lead epic retreats and experiences around the world with other incredible entrepreneurs, fulfilling his passion for adventure and beauty while inviting other talented individuals to experience more of the same.

By the end of this book, when you've completed the exercises, I promise that you, too, will have that kind of insight as to how to build your career or your business in a way that best positions you for success, personally and professionally, while minimizing your chances for failure. You will have conquered the toughest battle, the battle within. But, since life never stops, there will always be another battle around the corner. Growth must continue.

This is a never ending journey: to know thyself is not a one-time exercise.

Be a master student of yourself for a lifetime. You will thank me, but more importantly, your significant other, the people you work with, and your bank account will thank you for putting the intentionality into being a student of yourself.

> *"The paradox seems to be, as Socrates demonstrated long ago, that the truly free individual is free only to the extent of his own self-mastery. While those who will not govern themselves are condemned to find masters to govern over them."*
> —Steven Pressfield[21]

---

21   Pressfield, *The War of Art*.

unique talents

THE PERSONALITY TESTS

"Man's mind stretched to a new idea never goes back to its original dimensions."
—Oliver Wendell Holmes[22]

Some people fall into the pessimism camp when it comes to taking personality tests. "They're bogus," some people think. "They can be slanted to get what you want."

Or, they think, "Personality is adaptable and changeable—someone can become whatever they want. "

They're both right. People can slant tests to get the result they want and personalities *can* change a bit over time. But that's not the intent. When you answer the tests honestly, you'll find that they tend to reveal your strengths and weaknesses with remarkable

22   Oliver Wendell Holmes, *The Autocrat of the Breakfast-table* (London, UK: Low, Marston, Searle & Rivington, 1891), 266.

accuracy. You'll find little variance in the results even if you take the tests again, years or decades later.

I can slant the results of my test and I can learn most anything if I set my mind to it, but some things come to me much easier than others. Can I learn how to do the splits? Yep. Do I want to? Hell no! I never could come close to doing that in my most flexible of days as a boy in gymnastics class. But I know it's theoretically possible that I could become dramatically more flexible if I focused every day on stretching and increasing my flexibility.

My wife can very naturally and easily do the splits. She has more natural flexibility—a ballerina and dancer's body. She could go six months without stretching and then drop down and do the splits.

One of my nicknames in freshman year of college was Beefcake. I was a chiseled muscle machine with 6% body fat. Tight, strong, and dense. Flexibility was not my strength. Speed, power and agility were. If you asked me to do the splits then or now, I would slide about halfway down then topple over once I lost my balance, coming nowhere close to getting my legs all the way to the ground in the splits position. I could stretch daily for six months and never quite get there.

Each personality test provides different clues. Imagine you've been blind since birth. You are brought in to touch the leathery skin of an animal. You have no idea what you're touching other than it's leathery, it's thick, it's tough. You only get to touch one part of the animal.

Do you know what it is?

As likely as not it could be one of a dozen or more different animals.

Now, imagine if you were brought to the side of the animal and you were able to touch its toenails and its feet. Another clue.

Now imagine you went to the back of the animal and they let you touch its short and not very hairy tail. That just ruled out the Komodo dragon. Do you know what animal it is yet? You might be able to guess but it could still be a variety of animals.

You have another clue, but you're still far from the full picture.

Finally, if I take you to the front and allow you to touch the animal's massive horn and you can feel its powerful head do you know what it is?

A rhino of course.

But you still don't know what type of rhino it is. You don't know the sex, the temperament, or the health of the rhino.

Each piece brings clues. The more clues you have, the clearer your vision.

Figuring out who you are and what you're made for is far more complicated than figuring out what type of animal the blind person is touching.

That's why this is a lifetime journey. You're always changing and growing, though you have a general direction. The ground beneath your feet is always shifting. The world keeps spinning. Your body is creating millions of new cells every minute and millions are dying every minute. Growth is endless, so commit to the lifetime journey.

Is there some overlap? Yep. That's confirmation, and that's good. Will there occasionally be contradiction and will parts of the test be off? Yep. Remember, you're not going to be 100% this personality type or that type. You might be leaning 56% here or 83% there.

Use discernment, use practical wisdom to interpret the findings. You fall on a spectrum that can be adjusted somewhat based on your circumstances, though everyone has a home base.

One of the beautiful aspects of many of these tests is that they also show you your primary and secondary types. For example, in wealth dynamics I'm primarily a "creator." Having a burst of relevant and potentially transformative ideas is easy for me. VIP clients pay me a lot of money for that. I might have 19 projects open at once and many more ideas, business ventures, books, and partnerships that I'm biding my time to start.

But I also have a natural proclivity for making things systematic, orderly, and seeing how to organize ideas. Those tendencies come from my secondary side as a "mechanic" in the wealth dynamic test. I can lean into my mechanic side for a short burst, but I can't stay there for nearly as long or as easily as my ideation side without tremendous discipline, focus, and concentration.

When I reflect back to my season of divine storm when I reflected deeply on my zone of genius, I realized that I am one of the best at galvanizing ideas and momentum in a venture. And while I understand deeply how to manage and create systems, I'm nowhere near being one of the best in the world at managing a growing business. That's far outside my zone of genius and attempting it will get me into increasingly hot water the larger a business gets. Having experienced that painful season of heartache and setbacks, I don't want to return there, so in all future seasons I will design my ventures in a way that keeps me out of the administrative leadership roles. That's the gift of this process you're embarking upon: clarity.

Is this making sense?

Things will start to click even more as you go forward. Trust the process, knowing you don't have to understand everything. When you get in a Tesla, you may not understand how the car can propel you from zero to 60 in 2.7 seconds. But you press on the pedal and it will do it.

Together, the different personality tests will give you great insight into your unique talents. Each talent breaks down into three traits:

1. It's a superior ability that is valuable and noticeable: one talent for me is an ability to help entrepreneurs and leaders gain massive clarity in a short amount of time regarding who they are and what they are meant to do.

2. It energizes you: Your passion and enthusiasm is stoked when you use this skill. For me it's an ability to ideate and connect the dots, architecting a business concept or someone's next steps to get where they want to go or to get unstuck.

3. There's no ceiling: You could grow in this area endlessly and you are hungry to do so. For example, I love to grow and stretch my ideation capabilities and to swim and expand in the world of ideas.

One note before we dive into the tests: There are many powerful tests out there, and there is no way I could include them all in this book. Those that I have included are the ones I have found most valuable. If you have another test you love, go ahead and take it and let it add insight into your results.

So let's briefly break down each test:

WEALTH DYNAMICS: I love this test. My favorite. It connects you with and gives you an in-depth report of one of eight profiles that show you your natural pathway to building wealth, the risks and temptations you'll face, and how to manage your path to success.

KOLBE A™ INDEX: The Kolbe Index (Instinct Test) is unique. It does not measure intelligence, personality, or social style. It measures the instinctive ways in which you take action when you strive. Your result will describe your natural strengths—your modus operandi (MO).[23]

DISC: This is a behavior assessment tool based on the theory of psychologist William Moulton Marston,[24] which centers on four different personality traits: Dominance (D), Influence (I), Steadiness (S), and Conscientiousness(C).[25]

16 PERSONALITY TYPES: Built on the base of the Meyers Briggs test, this gives you a unique foundation and insight into who you are, how you're wired, and how you relate. This is the test that has popularized the introvert vs extrovert/feeler vs thinker discussions and awareness.[26]

CLIFTONSTRENGTHS STRENGTHS FINDER: This is based on 25 years of research by psychologist and father of

---

23 Kolbe A™ Index, Kolbe Corp, homepage, https://www.kolbe.com/kolbe-a-index/.

24 William Moulton Marston, *Emotions of Normal People* (London, UK: Kegan Paul, Trench, Trübner & Co., 1928), https://archive.org/details/emotionsofnormal032195mbp/mode/2up.

25 "The DISC Assessment," Tony Robbins, accessed April 19, 2021, https://www.tonyrobbins.com/disc/.

26 "Personality Types," 16Personalities, accessed April 19, 2021, https://www.16personalities.com/personality-types/.

strengths psychology, Don Clifton, who has focused on studying what is right with people and developing those talents to maximize potential. It measures the presence of talent in 34 areas, called themes, using 177 questions.[27]

I promise you, knock out all of these tests, read the results, take notes on yourself, and your understanding of who you are and what were made for will expand hugely.

When I went through the tests, I had confirmation and clarity that I am incredible at generating ideas, seeing the 30,000-foot view, thinking strategically about a brand or business, and galvanizing momentum in a project. I build deep, lasting relationships that go far beyond the surface level. I also end up getting very bored with a project or idea once it stabilizes or heads toward completion—hence, don't let me project manage much.

I would also make a horrible accountant or bean counter. You want me to follow a repetitive, rigid system like a McDonald's franchise? I'd rather have my toenails pulled out one by one while having my ears tickled. You want me to pour over mountains of data to make an effective decision? Lay me on my back and pierce my skin with tiny needles tipped with cayenne pepper and lemon to make my skin burn and burn.

The tests showed me where I'm a badass, but also where I'm a suckass. It's vital to know both.

The tests will give you massive numbers of clues and will provide confirmation of both your strengths and your weaknesses. Are you

---

27 "CliftonStrengths: Transform Great Potential Into Greater Performance," Gallup, accessed April 19, 2021, https://www.gallup.com/cliftonstrengths/en/253715/34-cliftonstrengths-themes.aspx.

ready to dive into discovering more about your personality types and your zone of genius?

Let's go!

action item:

Knock out the tests now!

DISC Self Assessment:
    www.tinyurl.com/GeniusDiscAssessment
Gallup Strengths Finder:
    https://www.gallup.com/cliftonstrengths/en/home.aspx
Meyers Briggs:
    www.tinyurl.com/GeniusMeyersBriggs
Wealth Dynamics:
    www.tinyurl.com/GeniusWealthDynamics
Kolbe A Index:
    www.tinyurl.com/GeniusKolbe

"To the dull mind all nature is leaden. To the illumined mind the whole word burns and sparkles with light."
—Ralph Waldo Emerson

unique life experiences

Your unique life experiences are your defining moments. These are Michael Jordan's moments of not making his high school basketball team,[28] hitting the game-winning shot as a freshman at UNC,[29] and also the less-heralded moments of his parents instilling the values of hard work and responsibility.

Everything in life happens for a reason and your life is littered with clues.

Let me take a moment to share how my own unique life experiences have paved the way for this book and for you and I to be connecting right now as an illustration. It might give you some ideas about what clues you should be paying attention to in your own life. As you read about me, I want you to ponder what life experiences you've had that are paving the way for your own unique zone of genius. Sound good?

I grew up on a horse farm, the oldest son of a father who was a German immigrant with an eighth grade education, and a mom

28   "Michael Jordan Didn't Make Varsity—At First," Newsweek, October 17, 2015, https://www.newsweek.com/missing-cut-382954.

29   Kyle Boone, "March Madness: Remembering when Michael Jordan hit the title-winning shot for UNC in 1982," CBS, March 18, 2019, https://www.cbssports.com/college-basketball/news/march-madness-remembering-when-michael-jordan-hit-the-title-winning-shot-for-unc-in-1982/.

who grew up on a Kentucky tobacco and livestock farm who became a teacher. So, I came from a middle-class American family with some European roots. My dad really enjoyed sports and could have played pro golf or pro tennis in Germany if he had stuck with it, but he grew up in post WWII Germany; times were lean to the point where his family would have meat once a week and potatoes, bread, and veggies the rest of the time.

As I grew up I developed a grit, a determination, and a fascination with sports and loved playing baseball, football, and basketball. I had a goal of being a pro baseball player one day. I remember days of gnarly double headers in 95-degree heat, grinding through brutal moments of fighting through a game on shear adrenaline and willpower. My dad knew hard work and mental toughness. We bonded over that.

Partly because of my childhood and the respect I developed for athletes and the mental battle and character development that happens in sports, I am planning on being the owner of a professional sports team by the time I'm in my 50s.

On the other hand, my mom wanted me to be a teacher like her. I actually started to fill out the paperwork for being a substitute teacher, but I immediately found myself overwhelmed with the bureaucracy of it all and dropped it. I thought I might one day be a college professor because I needed much more freedom and I enjoyed sharing wisdom and mentoring.

I loved leading retreats when I was president of my college ministry, a faith-based campus organization. As I started different businesses and learned more about the power of synergy and connectedness in leadership teams, I found myself leading retreats for my teams. I loved the retreats and the teams loved them as well.

We felt more connected and aligned when we had collectively experienced the mastermind effect.

Fast forward a few years, 16+ businesses later, lots of epic failures, and some flashy successes, I now have the joy and pleasure of creating dynamic, transformative retreats where leaders, creators, and entrepreneurs from around the country—and even some from other countries—journey in for a transformative experience.

I mentor typically 50+ entrepreneurs at a given time in the e-commerce field, the expert-driven coach/thought leader field, or the VIP one-on-one setting. I love what I do and I have a vision and a goal to establish myself as America's top entrepreneur mentor by the age of 50. I love the game of business but I especially love unleashing the talent and potential of the people who have their necks on the line with building their businesses.

We each have our part to play in charting our life experiences, but when we examine our unique life experiences in detail, we'll find more clues, more parts of the rhino (or elephant). Do you see how some clues were planted for both the teaching/mentoring side and the competitive sports front in my life? Our life experiences give us clues and that's why a thorough inventory of your unique life experiences will point toward your present and your future.

God—or the universe—doesn't waste anything.

So go back to your beginning. Starting from when you were a small child and right on up to the present moment, what experiences have you had that have shaped you? Wins, failures, experiences, adventures, harrowing moments, or extraordinary moments. Find those defining moments of your life. They offer clues, and compiling the clues will help you piece together the wonderful puzzle that is you.

action item

Take out the worksheets and complete the exercise of writing out your unique life experiences. Take full inventory of everything that comes to mind that is a distinguishable piece of the puzzle. *Do this in an inspired, minimally distracting place. Make a timeline of your life so you can later pull out your unique timeline and defining moments.

key relationships

LIFE AND DEATH

"You are the average of the five people you spend the most time with."
—Jim Rohn, author, speaker, mentor to Tony Robbins[30]

Your key relationships indicate some natural proclivities and some life path indications. Kobe Bryant's father was an NBA player for many years. Kobe was exposed to the game played at its highest level as a young boy and seeds of his future greatness were planted in him then.[31] The sons of major league baseball players are dramatically more likely to make it to the majors.[32] Elon Musk,

---

30 Aimee Groth, "You're the Average of the Five People You Spend the Most Time With," Business Insider, July 24, 2012, https://www.businessinsider.com/jim-rohn-youre-the-average-of-the-five-people-you-spend-the-most-time-with-2012-7.

31 Robin Cortez, "Joe Bryant Began an NBA Legacy That Changed Kobe's Life Forever," Sportscasting, April 5, 2020, https://www.sportscasting.com/joe-bryant-began-an-nba-legacy-that-changed-kobes-life-forever/.

32 Travis Sawchik, "MLB Is Increasingly A Father-Son Game," FiveThirtyEight, March 26, 2019,

Steve Wozniak, Steve Jobs, and Bill Gates enjoyed being around the nerdy computer crowd at a young age and eventually became some of our greatest tech geniuses of the modern era.

Let's ponder for a moment that some of your relationships and connections (even ones you barely know, or people you're one relationship removed from) all give clues about who you are and what you're meant to do. Your relationships open the door to a world of possibilities, opportunities, and indications of where you have support and inherent acres of diamonds beneath your feet that you might want to mine.

Do a quick assessment. Ask yourself these questions:

1. Who are the people who make me feel expanded and who infuse my spirit with life when I'm around them?

2. Who do I want to know more deeply when I tap into my heart and intuition?

3. Who do I want to eliminate or reduce exposure to? Who are the groups of people that bring me the feeling of death when I'm around them? Why?

4. Where do I have strong relationships that I haven't recognized or valued?

5. What patterns am I starting to see as I answer the questions above?

As you do this, you'll find clues about the people you'll want to intentionally spend more time with and the groups that you'll want to nurture. Some groups are more a part of your past: they served to help you become who you are, but they are not part of your future.

As you do your self-assessment of relationships, some of you may initially find that you don't have many key relationships. That's okay. You have some, plus there are other people you've crossed paths with and want to connect with and want to build a relationship with. That's what we're looking for.

Some of you may find that you have an abundance of relationships and if that's you, then start categorizing them by groups, but especially notice the least valuable and most valuable groups. Double down on the highest value groups, the ones that bring you the most life and eliminate or reduce the ones that are the least fulfilling.

When I first did this exercise, I started noticing that I have many relationships in the author and thought-leader world. Good friends like six-time author Jeff Goins, NY Times best-selling authors Rory Vaden and Dan Miller, and other writers are in my sphere. I also happen to have married an incredible writer and poet, Seven Sinclaire. I love spending time with those who love to discuss ideas. I feel so energized after hanging with them.

In addition to the thought leaders, I noticed I had a second group of e-commerce entrepreneurs and I loved that game too. I have friendships with people behind uber-successful e-commerce businesses like Colin Wayne of Redline Steel, Josh Axe of Ancient Nutrition, and Marshall Morris of iheartdogs.com. I love talking, connecting, and hanging with guys like that.

At the time when I first tried this exercise myself, I was primarily in the real-estate world. While I deeply appreciate the value that real estate investors, realtors, and real estate professionals bring to the world and the role they have played in my development, that world no longer brought me nearly as much joy, nor did swimming with the people who are primarily in that world.

I longed to swim in the world of ideas, the world of unlimited creation, and scalable e-commerce businesses which also have a much greater ceiling of possibilities.

So what clues are you finding? Share with me and others the clues you're finding. I'm truly curious to know what's showing up.

action item:

Complete the relationship inventory and examine it for patterns as you do a deeper dive into it.

passions and values

"We are shaped and fashioned by what we love."
—Johann Wolfgang von Goethe

The last step of the zone of genius process—passions and values—acts primarily as a filter that helps you discern where to invest your precious time and energy. Your passions are what get you excited and where you have a natural interest and joy. Your values indicate what you will stand for and what you stand against.

Passions are the things that make you come alive and give you a bottomless thirst for more. I could study entrepreneurship, human psychology, history, and marketing endlessly and my insatiable curiosity would only grow. When I was a freshman in college, I saw someone with a shirt that said, "So many books to read, so little time." I thought to myself, "Yep, that's true!" And I was secretly coveting that shirt though I would never wear it in public.

A passion is something you could study or work at throughout your lifetime and never get enough of. Passion projects raise your spiritual purpose, energy, and inspiration. When something stokes the flames of your passions, you find a swell of enthusiasm, ideas, and curiosity. You may find yourself stepping into a flow state because of the subconscious merger of work and play.

Values and passions that propel you toward something that's bigger than yourself tend to draw out your highest genius. George Washington became a great leader because of his role in America's Revolutionary War, his passion for freedom from tyranny, and his belief in the potential of a government run by and led by the voice of the people.[33] Martin Luther King, Jr. gave his most compelling speeches because of the critical nature of the oppression he was fighting in the civil rights movement.[34] Scott Harrison has raised hundreds of millions of dollars for clean water initiatives with Charity Water because he found a passion that called forth his highest genius.[35]

Let's get more granular. As a child, I had a natural passion for sports and the challenge of competition. I had natural athletic ability, I was wiry and strong and I enjoyed the battle of competition, win or lose (though I liked winning far more).

I also really enjoyed exploring the deep questions of life—particularly in college—and I loved games of strategy whether board games or video games. Even now, I love Settlers of Catan; I break it out during gatherings with family and friends as often as possible. If you have inherent gifts of strategy, you might love it too. In addition, I'm passionate about the stimulation of adventure travel and of meeting new high-caliber people (this also explains

33 "Biography of George Washington," George Washington's Mount Vernon, accessed April 19, 2021, https://www.mountvernon.org/george-washington/biography/.

34 "Dr. Martin Luther King, Jr.," NAACP, accessed April 19, 2021, https://naacp.org/dr-martin-luther-king-jr-history/.

35 "Scott Harrison's (Charity Water) Story," Charity Water, accessed April 19, 2021, https://www.charitywater.org/about/scott-harrison-story.

why hosting/attending mastermind retreats and European/ international travel are so fulfilling to me).

I developed an early interest in learning and growth and a belief that I could learn most anything. (Thanks mom for getting me hooked on reading!) I particularly started to enjoy human psychology during my dating years, partly because I was pretty socially awkward and just outside of the cool circle in high school. I wanted to be less awkward and I wanted to be funny so I could have a girlfriend and cool friends.

One weekend, my fraternity had a ball. My date for the weekend and I weren't really hitting it off: maybe my 20-year-old self was clumsy and my serious intensity was a turn off. I don't know what I did or said, but I knew I flubbed yet another romantic opportunity; the girl had found me attractive physically but not alluring personally.

In my intoxicated sadness and anger, at about 12:14 in the morning I proceeded to the restroom. About a half dozen of my fraternity brothers were in there, talking and taking care of business. I proceeded to the nearest urinal, took care of business, flushed, and then in the midst of my romantic frustration, I proceed to attempt to rip the urinal off the wall.

As I've mentioned, my nickname at the time was Beefcake and I was as chiseled as I could be at that stage. Roaring my rage and ripping at the urinal with all my muscular physique, I couldn't get it to budge. And finally, with all my energy expended, I gave up in another round of defeat for the night.

Needless to say, my fraternity brothers found it hilarious. At our fraternity meeting the next evening, I listened to my bystander brothers tell the tale of the spectacle of my attempted but utterly ineffective Hulk moves on the urinal to 50 other fraternity brothers. Just a little more embarrassment because of my social clumsiness.

But embarrassment aside, it was also more fuel on the fire of my interest—my passion—for human behavior, relationships, and psychology, and I continued to study. I found it fascinating and I've read dozens and dozens of books and spent thousands of hours studying and developing greater understanding of human psychology, leadership, and motivation and have practiced cultivating emotional and relational intelligence ever since.

As my career evolved, I found I loved the freedom and autonomy of entrepreneurship, but I also appreciated the risks and heartaches entrepreneurs can go through (especially when failing occurs despite giving your every effort to succeed). It is what led me to create this book and the genius within process to help talented people like yourself find your lane and have fewer failures and more wins. That's my passion.

So, what are your natural passions and how do they intersect with your unique talents and the relationship circle you've built over the years? Take some time and write down the hobbies and things that have brought you joy, enthusiasm, or unending energy over the years. What insights, clues, or light-bulb moments happen when you do so?

Now, let's talk about values.

Values are different from passions, they're pillars of identity, of what your life is all about. They represent your character and how you are known to others based on where you will make a stand. They are a mix of both what you are for and what you are against.

A few of my values:

1. Life is an adventure and I'm destined to experience the richness of it. (Values don't all have to be boring.)

2. Business exists to first serve the world and make it a better place; profit is necessary for sustainability but it's secondary. Use your gifts and your opportunities to serve the world first, not primarily to feed your own ego. The greatest leaders among us are our greatest servants.

3. Create win-win situations and do business and life with people who feel the same way.

One of my chief values and motives is freedom and a sense of autonomy. Without it, I feel like a monkey in a cage when someone is restricting or trying to control me. With it, I'm alive and eager to explore the Earth and the tide of ideas as my playground.

Some values are strong non-negotiables. Others are strong preferences that you can tolerate for a season. For example, a value for me is love and kindness. Another one is green energy and renewing the Earth. If I worked as an executive for Tesla, love and kindness would not be a prominent value with Elon's famous and obsessive 100-hour workweeks, but the green-energy value would be. Ultimately though, because I value freedom and I've found my purpose in unleashing people's God-given talent, I wouldn't be happy in that kind of work for long.

Now, what are your values? What do you stand for? What do you stand against? As you start ideating on your values, begin by writing out single words that have meaning for you: love, courage, adventure, reliability, etc. As you write out the words, you'll come up with phrases and intentions that connect with them and that reflect what you're for and what you're against.

If you find yourself getting stuck, talk about it with one of your close friends, family members, or your lover. Ask what they see as your values. They will have some insights that you may have missed.

Be honest with yourself. There may be things that you want to say represent your values, but if you're really truthful with yourself, you know they are things you don't really care about. That's okay. You are on the hunt for the deepest understanding of what makes you uniquely you. Forget the shoulds. Embrace what is.

action item

Knock out the worksheet exercise on values and passions. Write out your first round with zero editing. Don't write and edit together. They are two different processes. Do a first round on values and passions, then come back afterward and edit and polish.

> *"When you set yourself on fire, people will come and watch you burn."*
> —John Wesley

the first genius blocker: lack of belief

"You can never become a great man or woman until you have overcome anxiety, worry, and fear. It is impossible for an anxious person, a worried one, or a fearful one to perceive truth; all things are distorted and thrown out of their proper relations by such mental states, and those who are in them cannot read the thoughts of God."
—Wallace Wattles, *The Science of Being Great*[36]

Poor belief in yourself is a sure recipe for playing beneath your potential. In fact there's probably no better recipe for shattering your potential and falling through the floor of your ability than a lack of belief in yourself.

And yet, self-doubt can be a healthy indicator of your talent too. Steven Pressfield writes in *The War of Art*, "Self-doubt can be an ally. This is because it serves as an indicator of aspiration.

---

36 Wattles, *The Science of Being Great*, 12.

It reflects love, love of something we dream of doing, and desire, desire to do it.»[37]

The reality is, nearly every single person gets their confidence rattled in a major way at one point or another. It's not whether it will happen, it's how you handle it.

One son can take an abusive father's demeaning taunts, internalize them, accept them as truth, and always live as a shadow of his self. Another son can take that same abuse and fuel it into the flames that drive him to make something of himself to prove his dad wrong.

How do you overcome a lack of belief in yourself?

First, reverse the belief.

Wait a minute. How do you just reverse the belief? Let me show you.

Author, speaker, and spiritual teacher Byron Katie created an incredibly simple and potent process of self-inquiry that she calls "The Work." You take a belief that you hold about yourself through these four questions and by the end, the belief is transformed.

First, identify what that belief is. For example, "I am doomed to always fail." Or, "I will never find and keep my soulmate."

Byron Katie's Four Questions (and one of my own)

1. Is it true?

2. Can you absolutely know that it's true?

3. How do you react when you believe that thought?

4. Who would you be without that thought?

---

37 Pressfield, *The War of Art*, 39.

5.   What if the opposite of that belief was true?[38]

This is powerful, so I want to walk you through a personal example. In 2018, my real estate business, my cash cow at the time, disintegrated 60 days before my wedding. In addition, I had a real estate flip that was way over budget and that was taking far too long. My fiancée and I had a beautiful wedding planned in Florence, Italy, our favorite city in Europe. My private lender ended up forcing the flip into foreclosure five months after our wedding, refusing to negotiate with me on repayment timeline. I ended up losing over $500,000 that year on those two setbacks alone. With massive wedding expenses, my financial life was in a free fall at a time when it was supposed to be one of my happiest times of my life.

With expenses piling up and cash flow dwindling down, I shifted deeper into a stressed state. I worked tireless 12-16 hour days, six days a week. I woke up with my arms tightly wrapped around my chest because I was so stressed.

My saving grace was my wife. In the midst of seemingly insurmountable tension and during that fateful argument in Florence after our wedding, when I was still in crisis mode working to salvage a doomed marketing and branding agency, she said, "Michael, the thing that people most want is your mind. That's why your mastermind members love your retreats. That's what your clients want more of—your mind." She saw my genius, she saw my zone before I did. But I didn't want to own and claim that one of my highest pathways was mentoring.

---

38   Byron Katie, *A Mind at Home with Itself: How Four Questions Can Free your Heart, and Turn Your World Around* (New York: HarperOne, 2017).

Let's pretend I internalized the belief that I'm a failure as an entrepreneur and businessman:

1. Is it true? Not really. When I look at all the other things I've accomplished, the businesses I've started, the track record I've had in helping people break through barriers and doubt, it's pretty remarkable.

2. Can I absolutely know it's true that I'm a failure as an entrepreneur? No. I've got a mix of successes and failures. Some ventures have worked well, others haven't and that's the nature of the game I'm playing.

3. How do you react when you believe that thought? I feel weak, defeated, and disempowered. My will to continue forward is shot.

4. Who would you be without that thought? I would see the setbacks as setups: chances to flourish, chances to grow, chances to help others avoid some of the same mistakes I made.

5. What if the opposite of the belief were true? The opposite belief is that I'm a success as an entrepreneur and businessman. When I believe that, beautiful and incredible things happen. In fact, three of the businesses that I have an equity slice in, that I was a first investor in, are now worth $18 million, $20 million, and over $60 million respectively. Plus, all the mistakes and lessons of that dismal season served to make me go deep, get clear on where my genius lies, and catapult me into the direction I really desired to go in anyhow.

"Obey your soul, have perfect faith in yourself. Never think of yourself with doubt or distrust, or as one who makes mistakes."
—Wallace Wattles[39]

As you release these thoughts, it's just as important to fill your mind with powerful, resourceful images and beliefs. Release the negative but fill with the positive. After you've released the negative, go on the hunt for anchor memories: moments when you shined, where you succeeded. You can anchor them to your subconscious by asking yourself, "What if this is really who I am at my best?"

This is part of what I help people do in my Claim Your Power NLP sessions: we release the old stories, energies, and traumas, and anchor you to your most powerful identity.

One Friday afternoon during the height of the Coronavirus pandemic fears and uncertainty in 2020, I took one of my VIP and mastermind members and friends, Jake Kauffman, through this process. In the session, we found the part of Jake that wanted to play small in order to protect him. If you've been hurt and those wounds haven't fully healed, then they will often control you until that wounded part is integrated. After we acknowledge the wounded part and integrated with it, we found a memory or moment where he played at his highest self. Then we anchored him to that higher self in the meditation and visualization by asking that higher self to lead his life, to drive the bus off his life from that point on. Further, we gave his higher self a name, a more powerful identity. Then, we helped him visualize and anchor in his highest and best self through a timeline exercise where he started from the

---

39 Wattles, *The Science of Being Great*, 26.

future achievement, and we worked our way back to the present moment, each key step along the way, visualizing as if his highest self was leading each step along the way.

The most effective visualizations need a deep anchoring in not just what you see, but what you feel and what you sense. It needs to be a multisensory experience so the more you engage all five senses in your visualization the better.

Now, back to Jake. He went from doubt and hesitancy in his abilities, to being unstoppable and having a record income week the following week when fear was rampant throughout the world. It helped catapult him to a record year far higher than he ever thought he'd hit in his first full year as an entrepreneur.

To anchor your powerful identity belief even more strongly, there are two additional things you can do. First, find an inspirational figure you want to model. Secondly, I encourage you to walk, talk, and think the way you imagine that person would. Then, visualize and meditate as if you are living with their energy and guidance.

Many years ago, Amanda, a social media influencer who is now a business mentor to thousands, came to me for help. When we started our session together to work on her message and her new season, she broke down in tears within the first 20 minutes. She felt completely stuck and paralyzed—trapped in her old identity as a fitness influencer, which didn't give her life anymore. At first, my thought was, "Crap! I've got a crying girl on my hands! How do I get her to stop?" One of a guy's most dreaded moments is making a girl cry.

Amanda wanted to do business mentoring. That was a big leap from fitness. I hadn't yet had the experience I have now, and my first thought was, "I'm not sure how I'm going to help her."

Then I remembered this visualization process I've been describing, which I hadn't used for at least four years. In that moment, I decided, "You know what, this just might work."

I assured Amanda that we could get her there. I led her to connect with her old voice and story, then guided her to create a cognitive appreciation and then separation from her old voice, asking her to visualize and experience what it would be like to be someone who was truly in command of her new voice.

Amanda mentioned Oprah as someone who owned her voice and her story. So I had Amanda visualize acting and speaking as if she were Oprah. I re-anchored her to speak and to see herself communicating as herself with that kind of ownership.

Two hours later, Amanda was completely unstuck, empowered, and excited about her future. She was on fire with her message that next year after finding her voice, and she expanded her business massively in the new direction, cresting north of seven figures for the first time.

The steps I took Amanda through became the basis of my Claim Your Power process. Now I've taken nearly 1000 people through it live, and hundreds more have used my Claim Your Power process on my YouTube channel.

"As he thinketh in his heart, so is he."
—Proverbs 23:7[40]

---

40   Proverbs 23:7, *New King James Version* (NKJV).

second genius blocker: fear and worry

"Let's not allow ourselves to get upset by small things we should despise and forget. Remember, life is too short to be little."
—Dale Carnegie[41]

How many dreams have been silently sabotaged by fear? How many times have you found yourself sitting on the sidelines of life, not seizing an opportunity, because of fear?

Are you paralyzed with fear? That can be a good sign. Fear can be good; like self-doubt, it's an indicator. Fear often tells you what you have to do.

You have two choices in how to manage your fear: You can let it sabotage you or you can let it fuel you. In the first choice, fear destroys you, tempting you to hide your power, to dim your light,

---

41   Dale Carnegie, *How To Stop Worrying & Start Living* (New York: Pocket Books, 1990).

afraid of how something might change you, or others' perceptions of you, or your own trajectory. Fear can cause you to walk away with your tail tucked between your legs. Or, in the second choice, fear can motivate you to defy the odds, to rewrite your story stronger and better when you run into the fear instead of running away.

As you face your fear and thrive, you find that you become a higher version of yourself because fear calls you to decision. The actions, fears, jabs, and worries of others will not sabotage you when you've already faced and stared down the fear in yourself.

> *"There is no such thing as a fearless warrior*
> *or a dread free artist."*
> —Steven Pressfield, *The War of Art* .

Worry is praying for what you don't want to happen. Worry is wasted emotion, energy, and distracted focus. Worry is the sister of fear: an incessant dwelling on the possibility of something going wrong.

But how do you release worry?

Shift your focus.

Easier said than done right?

True.

One tip I learned from my NLP training: when experiencing worry, be present with it. Acknowledge it. Thank the worry for its good intent. It just wants to be heard and understood—usually it has a good intent. It's usually trying to protect you from harm. By being present with worry, making it feel heard, and thanking it for its good intent, it can then be released because it is acknowledged.

Then you can ask it to go to the back of the bus instead of driving your life.

Recently, I was on a coaching call with one of my VIP clients, Patricia. She immediately started sharing how consumed she was by massive anxiety and frustration. She brought up a huge worry about her abusive ex-husband and whether he would honor his word. She talked about the stress he was causing her regarding their kids.

I took her through an exercise to help her reframe and regain power over her circumstance. After connecting her to her worry and fear, we dove into the meaning of the fear.

It went like this:

"Patricia, is your ex truly capable of disrupting your life or is he more of an annoying pest?"

"Hmmm, I guess he can't really hurt me anymore. He's just very frustrating. So he is a bit more like a pest."

"So what is a pest that can't really hurt you, but is a bit annoying? Perhaps a fruit fly?"

She cracked up. "Yes exactly! My ex is an annoying fruit fly!"

"Ha! Exactly. Now put his face on the body of a fruit fly and have him buzzing around, snacking on your bananas."

As Patricia did this, laughing uncontrollably for a moment—which totally changed her emotional association with her ex—she got connected to who he really is. She now had tremendous control over her emotions. He couldn't disrupt her life, her purpose, or her joy anymore. He might be annoying sometimes, but because the distinction shifted deep within her subconscious, she's now totally in control.

Patricia acknowledged the worry, saw its good intent (protection), and radically redefined the meaning and story of who he is in her life. Six months later, she still sees her ex as an annoying fruit fly incapable of sapping her joy. In fact she often laughs when she thinks about him as a fly. She's free.

You can be free of the control of worry and fear too. It's essential that you escape the insidious controlling nature of fear and worry in order to fully claim your power and own your zone of genius. Otherwise the world will be robbed of your deepest gifts.

"Why would I think about missing a shot I haven't taken?"
—Michael Jordan[42]

---

42   Michael Jordan in *The Last Dance*, dir. Jason Hehir, 2020.

third genius blocker: distraction

"Most people don't want to acknowledge the uncomfortable truth that distraction is always an unhealthy escape from reality."
—Nir Eyal[43]

We live in an era where every device in your house is buzzing, alerting, and drawing your attention, where social media companies deliberately seek to make you addicted to their platforms, where every company clamors for your attention and wants to draw you into their vortex.

The name of the game is distraction because the name of the game is attention. Everybody wants your attention. Forty years ago, if you went on a road trip, no one could get ahold of you until you got to your destination. Now, you have a precious device that

---

43   Nir Eyal, *Indistractable: How to Control Your Attention and Choose Your Life* (Dallas: BenBella books, 2019), 26

has hundreds of different tools, apps, and games to distract you, a device people can use to get ahold of you instantly at nearly all hours of the day. They expect to be able to reach you because they expect you to be attached to this device.

Distraction takes many forms, and while an addiction to the cell phone may perhaps be the most pervasive, another powerful distraction from our zone of genius is our acceptance of "the good." As author, lecturer, and business management consultant Jim Collins wrote, "Good is the enemy of the great."[44]

What you are good at can lull you into a safe comfort zone where you abdicate what you're truly exceptional at. Sometimes the roots are self-sabotage, fear of shining in all your glory, fear of upsetting the status quo, fear of becoming as great as you know you're meant to be.

While the world of choice has drastically expanded your freedoms and options, the overwhelming nature of all those options creates a whole other category of problems and can stagnate you with indecision. Author, lecturer, and investor Nir Eyal writes in his excellent book *Hooked*, "Too many choices or irrelevant options can cause hesitation, confusion, or worse—abandonment."[45]

How do you bust through distraction to do what you're truly meant to do?

First, ruthlessly eliminate distractions and create focus. Starve the things you want to see die, feed the things you want to live. Narrow your choices: you can't do everything at once.

Second, create rhythms and routines that help you focus on what's most vital, what truly is your zone of genius. For example,

---

44   Jim Collins, *Good to Great: Why Some Companies Make the Leap… And Others Don't* (New York: HarperCollins, 2011), 1.

45   Nir Eyal, *Hooked: How to Build Habit-Forming Products* (New York: Penguin, 2014).

I start my day off with my phone in airplane mode, not checking email, avoiding social media, and feeding my mind positively. This protects me from being yo-yoed by other people's demands and attention. I don't do work in the bedroom. I get up within the same hour-and-a-half range every day, even on most weekends.

Third, get your most vital—most powerful—work done first thing in the morning after you've done a short morning workout routine. For me that's ideally less than 30 minutes to get my body and mind in the right place. I learned this from best-selling author and business coach Craig Ballantyne, in his *Perfect Week Formula*.[46] In fact, because of my morning routine shift, I'm able to move high-level projects and opportunities forward during two to three high-value creative hours before most people are even up. That has halved the time it used to take me to accomplish significant projects.

Fourth, delegate, eliminate, or just stop doing the things that are not in your zone of genius. I don't mow the grass. I don't hang shelves. I don't do accounting or complicated software stuff. I avoid stuff I don't like and I'm not good at like the plague.

You and I have covered a lot in the arena of distractions and their sabotaging influence on your zone of genius. The three great blockers of your genius: beliefs, worries and fear, and distractions can all be dramatically reduced or eliminated in their influence in your life. Take action now and make powerful decisions while you're most motivated. Otherwise, you'll leave a lot of your genius on the sidelines of life, rotting and stinking up the world when it could have been put to good use.

---

46   Craig Ballantyne, *The Perfect Week Formula: Build Your Business Around Your Life, Not Your Life Around Your Business* (Early to Rise Publishing, 2019).

life or death

WHAT EXPANDS
OR CONSTRICTS YOU?

*"What we choose to focus on and what we choose to ignore
[defines] the quality of our life."*
—Cal Newport[47]

Years ago, in a mastermind group I led in Nashville, a friend of
mine, Jonathan Harris, shared a process that goes like this: You lay
out a sheet of paper and on one side you write the word "Life," and
on the other side, "Death." Then, under those headings, you write
out everything in your life that brings you life and everything that
brings you death. From the smallest of things to the largest.

Do a deep inventory of all the activities and all the things you
were part of in the last week, and the last month, that brought
you life. You might find yourself writing out things like delicious

---

47   Cal Newport, *Deep Work: Rules for Focused Success in a Distracted World* (New York:
     Grand Central Publishing, 2016).

food, a hot cup of coffee, reading an inspiring book, playing with your dog, connecting and ideating with another friend on the same path as you, tickling your children, daily walks with your lover, speaking to audiences, creating a new product—whatever comes to mind.

Then do the same kind of inventory for death. You might write: doing laundry, being in loud environments, feeling rushed, hanging out with the same people, certain family members, doing accounting, responding to emails, sitting through staff meetings.

The important thing is write out everything that comes to mind. No editing. You have to give your mind permission to share without a filter.

If you have the Zone of Genius Workbook, this is included as one of the exercises. The beauty of the exercise is that it allows you to gain significant insight when you see patterns around all the things that breathe energy into your life and all of the things that bring in death. The goal is that you will include more of the things that give you life in your schedule and get rid of the items that bring death.

As you work through the process, you start creating a breakdown of what you need to get off your plate, right now. You'll also see what you need to schedule and make more time for. When I have my clients break these down in my mastermind groups, the process creates immediate shifts and allows them to see where they need to let go of certain things and take hold of others, and where they've neglected themselves in the pursuit of building their business.

Once you are done with your life/death exercise, you'll have much greater clarity of where all your time and energy is going.

When you couple that with your deepest areas of gifting, I want you to then categorize your activities into the time quadrants of $10, $100, $1,000, and $10,000 per hour. Assign a dollar value for the activities you do based on either: A) The revenue you generate for that activity ($2,000 for prospecting calls). B) How much you'd have to pay someone to replace you doing that activity (e.g., video editing $50 per hour). Or put your own hourly value. But when you do this, you'll have much greater clarity on waste in your week and know where the biggest impact levers are in your business.

When I took one of my clients, Rob Murgatroyd, through a VIP one-day strategy session, we tackled the zone of genius and his hourly breakdowns. At the end of it, we realized he was making $2,000 an hour in his chiropractic business for the energy he was putting in. Not a bad hourly return. But at the end of the day, his real passion for the next season of his life was his *Work Hard/Play Hard* podcast and the dynamic adventure trips he created for his high entrepreneur clients.

Gaining clarity on what his chiropractic business produced for him gave him the fuel to pursue the next year of building his podcast while also keeping his primary existing business running strong until he was ready to part from it.

action item

Block off 30+ focused minutes to do your Life/Death Exercise. After you do this, take a few moments and see what can be done to schedule in more of your life-giving activities and delegate/delete/reduce your death-giving activities.

When you actually schedule these things in your life and business and reduce the death activities, you will find a surge of energy, an increase in joy, and more fulfillment. And guess what? Your whole day will change, which means your whole week will change, which means your years ahead will be different and your life forever altered because you have intentionally brought more of what brings you life and less of what brings you death.

After you do the life/death exercise, you'll want to do the hourly breakdown to get greater clarity of what activities you want to delegate or eliminate. The exercises are not meant to be hard and fast for eliminating everything that's a lower value activity, because some activities bring you life. For example, if walking your dog clears your head and rejuvenates you, then it's more emotionally valuable than the $15 an hour you could hire a daily dog walker for.

action item

Ideally, you'll want to do this exercise twice a year at a minimum to continue to build momentum in designing your life. Take action on the life/death exercise and make decisions through this filter and you undoubtedly will design out your life to be more and more fulfilling.

"The phrases that men hear or repeat continually, end by becoming convictions and ossify the organs of intelligence."
—Johann Wolfgang Von Goethe

power positioning statement

"Nothing great will ever be achieved without great men, and men are great only if they are determined to be so."
—Charles De Gaulle[48]

What is a power positioning statement? It's a clear compelling statement that distills the essence of your genius and demonstrates who you are and where your talents excel, so that you claim valuable real estate in your ideal customer's mind. When someone thinks of Mike Zeller, I want them to see him as America's top entrepreneur mentor. Am I internationally known as that? Not yet. In five years, it will be a different story. But that power positioning statement helps me anchor my identity and my vision now so that I take decisive steps to move in that direction.

You can have multiple power positioning statements, though one may be your primary public facing statement that you use the

48   Charles de Gaulle, *The Edge of the Sword* (Santa Barbara, CA: Praeger, 1975).

most. While I am establishing myself as America's top entrepreneur mentor, I am also building a secondary power positioning statement as a preeminent business architect. I want people to see that I'm brilliant at this and I can help some of the most talented people in the world design an incredibly fulfilling and aligned business and life around their unique zone of genius.

So how do you create a power positioning statement? This is one of the hardest parts of the process and one that I find my VIP and mastermind clients need the most help and support with. The reason is that it's hard to read the label when you're on the inside of the bottle.

Begin by writing out key words, key identities that you want to be known by, even if you're not there yet. I know I'm not known as America's top entrepreneur mentor yet, it's going to take years to create that reputation based on thousands of more results (maybe you'll be one of them). But I'm on my way. I know the vision I seek, I know the path I'm on. I know the results I'm creating right now for clients that are seeing me as an incredible entrepreneur mentor.

As you create your power positioning statement, know that it's going to go through several rounds before you land on the one you like the most right now. As you're ideating, test it out with friends and clients who know you well and who you think would give you insightful feedback. Bear in mind that you will also update this profile occasionally as time goes on as you gain a deeper sense of who you are and what your truest zone of genius is.

action item

Create your power positioning statement by first ideating on words that resonate with you and feel most true to who you are. Then combine them into phrases. Test out different sentence combinations to find something that flows. Value progress over perfection. This is part art, part science, and it's going to be a bit messy at the beginning. Share these power positioning statements in the FB group and tag me, @mikezeller, on all social media platforms as you share them. I want to see what you create and where you get stuck.

the rapid procrastination elimination process

THE 80% ADVANTAGE

"Only those who dare to fail greatly can ever achieve greatly."
—Robert F. Kennedy, Sr.[49]

Procrastination taunts us with her alluring voice. She lulls us to sleep with soft whispers, "Just wait till another day when you're ready. It will be better then."

Then her twin sister, perfectionism, slips in a word of confirmation, "Besides, you want to make it great anyhow. Wait till you can give it your all."

---

49   Robert F. Kennedy, "Day of Affirmation Address," Speech at University of Capetown, June 6, 1996, https://www.jfklibrary.org/learn/about-jfk/the-kennedy-family/robert-f-kennedy/robert-f-kennedy-speeches/day-of-affirmation-address-university-of-capetown-capetown-south-africa-june-6-1966.

Off to sleep you go. Two years later, the soul gnawing has gotten louder or, in some cases, more faint as you've become even more disconnected from your heart's purpose. Two more years have gone by that you can't get back.

You may find yourself distracted with other worthy endeavors that are good, but they aren't the great things that you know you're meant for. The good is the fiercest enemy of the great in our lives.

As I write this book, I am constantly tempted to work on programs and projects that are at least six months away from launching, which would further delay my progress on the book. Finishing this is my greatest project at hand and while there are other worthy endeavors to pursue, timing-wise, they're not right and they would only be a very tempting distraction. Personally, I find myself tempted by another shiny object (i.e., another opportunity), the latest cryptocurrency trend, or another idea even if I have a few too many ideas in the works already. Those are the more valuable distractions vs the temptations to read ESPN, scroll through social media, or hop into a political debate that will go nowhere.

What are the most tempting distractions that pull *you* away from what needs to be done right now?

Distractions are a form of resistance. Resistance has many faces and two of the best are: procrastination and perfectionism.

What you want to know is how to overcome procrastination on something you know is right up your alley. Something that truly is in your zone of genius and your core purpose. Creating and developing something new are among the hardest challenges we take on. In this world of rapid innovation and prototyping, accelerating change and developing businesses, projects, and ideas as fast and as high in quality as possible are paramount.

As a creative entrepreneur myself, and working with countless creatives as clients, business partners, friends, I end up getting stuck way too often in the cycle of procrastination and perfectionism. I especially find myself procrastinating on writing, on doing sales efforts, and developing compelling social media stories. Those are powerful levers that really move the needle for me, but it's more comfortable for me to mind map, read a book, or ideate on designing a worksheet or process.

All too often, brilliant people with incredible innovations and ideas get stuck before they even get started because of procrastination

Where do you tend to get stuck?

If you're like me and countless other entrepreneurs, our tendency is to get stuck before we begin. We procrastinate. We hold back on starting something because we're not sure how we'd solve it, who we'd need to do it, or even if we *can* do it.

Sometimes the thought of creating something up to your standard of excellence may also overwhelm you. If you somehow get the project off the ground, you may never actually release it because it may not meet your standards of perfection. There's always that next level of excellence that you're striving for before it's ready to be shared.

I like to think of procrastination and perfectionism as the sinister sisters. They scheme and trap us into languishing in the apathetic neutral ground of mediocrity all too often.

Let's define them. Perfectionism is languishing in indecision and a noncommittal status because something can't meet your standards. Procrastination is swimming in inaction.

Subtly, they masquerade as resistance. Resistance is that taunting presence that seeks to thwart any form of creative or entrepreneurial work, or really anything represents you becoming more of who you are meant to be. Creative work is so critical to our advancement as human kind, that it is also thwarted at nearly every step. But in overcoming the obstacles we become who we are meant to become as part of our own heroic journey.

When you are trapped in the non-virtuous cycle of procrastination and perfectionism, you might find your soul numbing, your energy sagging, and your temptation to distraction rising.

To become unstuck, you need to get moving in the right direction and operate with a different paradigm. Let's start with the new empowering paradigm.

Philosophical Paradigm Shift: Embrace the Suck until It Becomes Good

To remove the sinister sisters, several things need to take place, but first a new paradigm.

"At the beginning we suck. Then we suck a little less. Eventually we suck so little we actually become good."
—Garret J. White[50]

I cannot be afraid of sucking. In fact, part of me has to embrace it as part of my journey to suck less and eventually to becoming good, then great. Holding back because I suck at something doesn't work and doesn't serve me or the progress I seek.

---

50 Garrett J White, "Your life sucks because you suck…." Facebook Live video, accessed April 15, 2021, https://www.facebook.com/watch/live/?v=815837905617210&ref=watch_permalink.

Embracing the suck is perfectly paired with the second piece of the paradigm shift which is accepting that "done" is better than "perfect."

When you're done and released, you can get real feedback. With real feedback, you can make relevant improvements. With relevant improvements, you can test again. You can accelerate progress and testing.

Feedback is another name for failure. High performers who consistently operate from their zone of genius embrace this mentality. One of my favorite stories is of Sara Blakely, the billionaire founder of Spanx. At the dining table every week, her dad would ask her, "What did you fail at this week?"

After she shared her failures from the week, he would high five her.

In an interview for *Inc.,* Blakely explained, "I didn't realize it at the time how much this advice would define not only my future but my definition of failure. I have realized as an entrepreneur that so many people don't pursue their idea because they were scared or afraid of what could happen. My dad taught me that failing simply just leads you to the next great thing."[51]

So how do you apply this? Aren't there some instances where this mindset or paradigm has some drawbacks? Yes. Done isn't better than perfect in campaigns with huge implications or high regulatory fines at risk or where an entire enterprise can be undone with a single bad mistake or imperfect execution. In those cases, you're testing and embracing the suck before a product or offering is released to the public. So you're still utilizing the paradigm to

---

51   Melanie Curtin, "Billionaire CEO Sara Blakely Says These 7 Words Are the Best Career Advice She Ever Got," Inc., March 25, 2021, https://www.inc.com/cameron-albert-deitch/steve-case-arlan-hamilton-investor-funding-inc-vision-summit-2021. html.

move forward, you're just not releasing to the public yet because the cost of public failure is too great.

How do you avoid disaster? First, use wisdom in your testing and release of a project, campaign, offer, etc. For example, say you've got an email list of 100,000 and you want to test out a new potentially controversial offer. Don't send it out to your whole list. Send it to say 2,000 of your most forgiving audience to micro-test it, so the damage is minimal before you send to the whole list.

Second, test in ways in which you can recover. Doing 100 small tests is far better than one massive test. You'll have many more ideas for improvements from the 100 small tests. You want feedback and improvement as quickly as possible.

Let's summarize the philosophical paradigm shift:

1. Permission to fail forward faster; failure isn't failure, it's feedback.

2. Embrace the suck, which ensures that you move from suck-to-good-to-great faster.

3. Done is better than perfect (80% of the time).

Now, let's talk about the 80% Advantage and how it intertwines with the rapid procrastination elimination process.

The goal of the 80% Advantage is to get the first 80% of a project complete as fast as possible. Then it becomes easier to improve it another 80% and so on until you've done six rounds. Whatever you do, do not allow the energy, vision, or desire to get to 100% on the first round. It will slow down progress and hinder everything in a major way.

The Advantages:

If we stack the advantages of this process, it comes down to two central advantages that we all want more of:

1. Speed
2. Quality

Let's be real here, who doesn't want to get something done faster? And at a higher quality of a finished product?

This can represent further improvements to the project on your part or, even better, further improvements done by other talented people. Even though this is called "the second 80%," it actually brings the overall project to 96% of the ideal result. You will want to delegate the second 80% as much as possible.

Example: Here is how the 80% Advantage can look in writing a book or an article:

First 80%: I mind map the idea (five-10 minutes).

Second 80%: I talk it out loud on my phone and send it to my AI transcription service. (five minutes for $.50; delegating).

Third 80%: My writer expands on it and polishes it up (five minutes of direction, two hours of my writer writing).

Fourth 80%: I review it and make edits (five-15 minutes).

Fifth 80%: I review it again and ask for certain images or quotes included (five-10 minutes).

Sixth 80%: I approve it.

*One of my favorite activities with my team: set the vision and direction with them, then delegate the first draft. Thus, the first 80% is done collaboratively and they are empowered to do the next 80%. Once they complete that next version, then we'll meet.

action step

Take out the worksheet or, if you're working in your notebook, you can write out the following:

1. What is your next big initiative/project/idea/launch:

    _____

2. Whose help do you need on the project? List everyone that comes to mind, their role, and if you don't have the right person yet, identify the places you may be able to find them.

3. Let's remove procrastination and perfectionism by breaking down each 80%:

    First 80% _____
    Second 80%_____
    Third 80% _____
    Fourth 80% _____
    Fifth 80% _____
    Sixth 80% _____

How will it feel when you've completed each step?

Will this help you accomplish a more complete and developed project than you would have had otherwise?

Take action on moving through each phase of the 80%.

80/20
your zone of genius

"If we did realize the difference between the vital few and the trivial many in all aspects of our lives and if we did something about it, we could multiply anything that we valued."
—Richard Koch[52]

Management consultant Richard Koch wrote a seminal book that has forever altered the landscape of how we evaluate priorities, activities, and opportunities. The book I'm referencing is *The 80/20 Principle*, which has sold over 1.5 million copies to date. It is a must-read.

The original concepts were first popularized by an Italian economist, Wilfred Pareto, in the 1800s when he noticed a pattern that showed up repeatedly.[53] For example, 20% of people held 80% of

52 Richard Koch, *The 80/20 Principle: The Secret to Achieving More with Less* (New York: Currency, 1999).

53 Kevin Kruse, "The 80/20 Rule And How It Can Change Your Life," Forbes, March 7, 2016, https://www.forbes.com/sites/kevinkruse/2016/03/07/80-20-rule/?sh=516ee8f03814.

the wealth and roughly 20% of merchants produced 80% of the taxes. This pattern showed up enough that he discerned it must be an underlying principle and it became known as the Pareto principle until Koch made it even more mainstream.

The core principle is that 20% of activities produce 80% of the results and this is the typical pattern that shows up repeatedly in nature, in economics, and in our lives. The exact percentages can vary, but the point is it's always predictably unbalanced between input and output. It's never 50/50.

The 80/20 Principle asserts that a minority of causes, inputs, or efforts usually leads to a majority of the results, outputs, or rewards. Taken literally, this means, for example, that 80 percent of what you achieve in your job or business comes from 20 percent of the activities/time/energy spent. Thus, four-fifths of the effort is largely insignificant.

To illustrate how this applies, let me share a story from my life. One weekend, several years ago, I went to a church service on a Sunday morning. I show up at this church thinking I was going to experience the usual round of worship, a good message, the normal meet-and-greet, and then the request for the offering. Instead, a few minutes after everyone settled in, the pastor and the leaders ushered us to the homeless shelter across the street because this was a day when we were doing church service by serving people in need. Good idea and concept.

As we headed across the street, I quickly saw that we had more church people than homeless people. Some were assigned hotdog cooking duties, others were serving plates, and many of us were standing around aimlessly trying to figure out what to do. I didn't want to waste the opportunity, so I went in search of some homeless guys to talk to and encourage. I found three teenage guys who were already talking to other church members. I joined in and did my best to have an impactful and minimally awkward conversation with these guys for 20 minutes before I ran out of stuff to say or questions to ask.

I departed feeling disappointed. I hadn't really used my gifts nor had I made a meaningful difference. Good intent by the church but incredibly difficult to execute. And it reminded me why I dislike volunteering, at least in the typical sense. You end up feeling like you're just a warm body vs making a deep and lasting impact in a way that only you could do.

A few months went by and I was at another church. The pastor announced their Christmas extravaganza and how they were looking for warm bodies, I mean volunteers. I thought to myself, "No way I'm volunteering for Christmas. That's death by 1,000 cuts for me." But, I believe in being a giver and helping out those that are less fortunate. Quickly, I realized something that would be cool. At that time I had a car dealership, Providence Auto Group. We had a give-back campaign where every car we sold helped us to give another car to a family in need and we partnered with nonprofits to support their efforts. I wrote down on the Christmas volunteer card, "We would be willing to give a car away to a family in need for Christmas."

I left my email and phone number and two days later I got an email and we coordinated with Crosspoint to give a nice minivan to a family desperately in need during the church's Christmas extravaganza. It was a beautiful highlight of their Christmas special that was seen by 20,000 people and it inspired others to think and give generously. We helped out a family in need in a way that was deeply aligned with our own mission. We were uniquely positioned to help out in a very special way, which was far more impactful than my volunteering for three frustrating hours moving boxes, serving food, or awkwardly having small talk. The deeper desire in volunteering or doing most any other activity especially of the altruistic nature is to make a difference, to feel needed. Volunteering is wonderful when you feel needed, when you feel like you truly helped. But without that, it may feel like a waste in today's overly busy world.

Our Christmas gift brought us goodwill, enabled us to fulfill a central part of our mission and attracted more customers to us in a way that wouldn't have happened otherwise. The gift illustrates the principle of imbalance: a handful of decisions or actions will have disproportionate results.

Koch advocates, "Do only what you are best at and enjoy the most. Calm down, work less, and target a limited number of very valuable goals where the 80/20 Principle will work for us, rather than pursuing every available opportunity."[54] He concludes, "The 80/20 Principle suggests…that we are actually awash with time and profligate in its abuse.»[55]

Let's break down how the 80/20 rule works with your zone of genius. In your career, in your business, about 80% of the results will come from 20% of your effort or 20% of your activities. One of the secrets of highly effective people is that they focus a lot more time and energy on the top 20%. Your zone of genius is in the top 20%. Hence, why at this point, you've likely spent many hours getting greater clarity on your zone of genius.

---

54   Richard Koch, *The 80/20 Principle: The Secret to Achieving More with Less* (New York: Currency, 1999), 39.

55   Ibid, 19.

What would it look like for you to first gain tremendous clarity on your top 20%? Secondly, what would it look like to design your business, your life around that and delete, delegate, or minimize much of the 80%?

As you have gained increasing clarity around your unique gifting during this zone of genius process, you can now utilize the 80/20 principle as an additional filter to make decisions through that will further reinforce your value, your gifting and your impact.

For example, part of my core role and the core value I provided to my partners at Providence Auto Group was that I designed much of the brand identity from the messaging standpoint and helped architect the customer experience and the give-back story. In addition, I led team retreats initially, which helped give us the courage to get the business off the ground. I was able to utilize my genius in multiple ways.

Nathan McCauley, one of the partners, was brilliant as a car buyer, knew the car business incredibly well, and had a terrific artistic touch that elevated the brand identity. Simon Lawrence, our third partner, was very gifted at driving sales, creating enthusiasm, and being the face of the brand and customer experience. When our business was at its peak, we each were playing most deeply in our zone of genius.

Now that you've gone through your zone of genius exercise and you have a basic understanding of the 80/20 principle, how do you apply all this together?

action items:

First, write down the 10 most valuable activities that bring the most impact to your job or business that you do. After assessing that list, decide on what the top two most important activities are, the real needle movers. This will be hard to decide and you may have a toss-up between a couple.

Now, what impact would it have to double your energy and focus in those top two areas? Figure out how to double the amount of energy and time you focus on those top two areas, schedule them in during peak energy and focus hours and watch your business really move.

> *"God plays dice with the universe. But they're loaded dice. And the main objective is to find out by what rules they were loaded and how we can use them for our own ends."*
> —Joseph Ford[56]

*Providence Auto Group: I sold out my equity in 2017 and the business closed in 2018. but we had a run as being the only socially minded car dealership in the Southeast. My business partners, Simon Lawrence and Nathan McCauley, were good friends and partners and we are proud to have given away almost $300,000 worth of vehicles to people in need while we were open while also creating one of the highest rated car buying experiences in the Southeast. Most of our recipients never had a driver's license before that moment as they didn't think it'd be possible. Their lives were

---

56   Joseph Ford as quoted in James Gleick, *Chaos: Making a New Science* (New York: Penguin, 2008), 314.

forever changed and those have been some of my proudest moments as an entrepreneur. Note, I fully flexed and utilized my zone of genius as a business architect and entrepreneur mentor in the creation of this business and it was a great learning ground for me.

what do i do with my zone of genius?

"What you can do, or dream you can, begin it. Boldness has genius, power, and magic in it."
—Johann Wolfgang von Goethe[57]

You've done all this hard work to know yourself better. You've accumulated more data, more insight, more reflection, more self-discovery in this burst of focus on the most marvelous person in your life, you. Now what do you do with it?

First, keep the perspective that this is a lifelong journey, not a destination. You gathered a lot of clues about you during this process. The clues will lead to deeper alignment when you use them effectively. The most fulfilling moments in my life have been when I've been most deeply aligned. My most frustrating mo-

---

57 Johann Wolfgang von Goethe; John Anster, trans., *Faustus: A Dramatic Mystery* (London, UK: Longman, 1835), 15.

ments when I've been most deeply out of alignment. I know that's true for you too.

If you've made it this far, and you've done all the work, I absolutely salute you. If you haven't done the exercises, stop reading right now and go back and do them as they are what will change your life.

Second, assuming you've done the exercises, you can communicate much more clearly where you're amazing and where you suck. Do whatever you can to stay in the amazing lane and avoid the suck lane. Avoid letting someone talk you into doing work in which you suck.

Third, you now have a much clearer filter on your unique talents, your key life experiences, your unique relationships, and your values and passions. Use it to gauge your decisions, especially your most critical decisions. Our destiny is made in our decisions.

Having led hundreds of people through this process, I've found that people usually fall into one of the two camps. Many have massive leaps in clarity right away, even just from taking the tests. They love the insights they have, and they quickly make significant shifts in how they relate, how they communicate, how they lead, and how they create in their work and their personal life. The process helps them name their giftedness, where they shine and how they make their biggest impact.

Others will have more challenges understanding how to make sense of it all. You might be in the second group, where you are still a little bit confused about your zone of genius. That's okay. I didn't understand a lot of my results and what they meant initially. As time went on, though, and I continued to notice clues and reflect, patterns and insight emerged.

"We can only connect [the dots] looking backwards."
—Steve Jobs[58]

Both camps are okay and you may experience a bit of both. No matter where you're at, keep moving forward. Each step you take shows you the next step.

This process is meant to show you some of your next steps, but it's not meant to show you your whole life-path, nothing can do that. It will help you envision your big picture of what you're creating and who you're becoming, but that does not mean that it can lay out the whole pathway for you.

Here are some of the things I want you to do:

I want you to begin discussing your new insights with safe, supportive people in your life. That may include your significant other, your coworkers, friends, family, or other mentors. Getting feedback can provide confirmation or redirection if you're off on something. Remember, this is not an exact science. It's part science, part art. If someone is going to be jealous or judgmental in their response, it's likely best not to share or ask for their feedback. They might cast doubt and dim your light.

I have gone through this process with hundreds of high-achievers of all backgrounds, from NFL players, to moms, to talented entrepreneurs just starting out or doing eight figures. Every one of them gains greater insight, and more often than not, massive breakthroughs that unpack over the months and the years ahead.

Through this process, you will know how to lead, how to set up your life, and how to set up your business or your role within your

---

58 "Text of Steve Jobs' Commencement address (2005)," Stanford News, accessed April 15, 2021, https://news.stanford.edu/2005/06/14/jobs-061505/.

job, so that you can stay in the lanes you flourish in. You will begin to see how to live more richly and impact more deeply.

You may discover that you are out of alignment with things that are a passion and fulfilling for you. Your soul may long for something more attuned to your passion, your gifting, and the person you are uniquely meant to be. Recognizing these things will help to give you clarity on your next steps for getting closer to where you should be, but don't expect to arrive there overnight.

In your personal life and with your family, your relationships with your kids or parents, you will find that you can communicate more clearly about who you are, what you're about, what brings you life, and what brings you death.

The zone of genius process helps people make sense of you, it helps *you* make sense of you. And it helps you make sense of others.

As human beings, we have the tendency to project onto others what we want them to be or how we see ourselves instead of appreciating their differences and their uniqueness. By learning your zone of genius, your judgment of others will decrease and your appreciation will increase. That means you'll be able to love more freely, more authentically, and in a more aligned way. You'll see how truly special you are but also how truly special others are as well.

Lastly, I want to ask and challenge you to take out your calendar and schedule dates three months from now, six months from now, and one year from now, to review your answers and your worksheets. You'll move forward and take greater steps into your zone or genius over the next six months, and when you look back, that will be clear. When you review these notes again, you'll notice new things that you didn't see that first time. You'll see which things are working out, your progress, your lack thereof, and you'll be able to course correct and step more deeply into who you're really meant to be.

Invite others to go along with you and discover their genius. After my wife and I celebrated our wedding with family and friends, Cyrus Gorjipour, the co-founder and CEO of Goalcast mentioned to me, "Mike, it's crazy. Everyone we talked to at your wedding knew *all* their personality types!"

Well, they knew their personality types because if you're in my vortex for long, I will invite you into knowing yourself better. Get yourself more aligned and you'll see your fulfillment, your impact, and eventually your income rise in most cases.

Invite others to go through the same process with you. I promise you, you will create more richness in your relationships, more power, more confidence, and more wisdom. And as you do, share all these with me: I want to know, because I want to make this process even better. I want to make it even more powerful. And I want to help even more people find their unique purpose on this planet with love, kindness, and greatness. Find me on Instagram: @themikezeller.

Before we go, let's talk about hobbies and side interests. Your hobbies will often indicate some natural passions and sometimes may even indicate the deepest and most authentic part of your genius. Elon Musk and Jeff Bezos were both fascinated with space and had side-hustle hobby interests in space. Now they both have invested billions in their space companies and are revolutionizing a new frontier.[59] [60]

Create space for your natural interests and hobbies without letting them consume you. Side interests are a great place to cultivate your talents and to experiment with other parts of your gifting that wouldn't necessarily be used for financial compensation in the job. But do not ignore hobbies, because aspects of them might develop in a way that becomes immeasurably valuable at another point.

My Zone of Genius Date

Three months into dating the lovely girl who would eventually become my wife, I asked this beautiful and wonderful human, who was very different from me, to take a bunch of personality tests. I framed it as, "Let's discover each other's uniqueness more." She readily agreed. She took most of the tests that are in the zone of genius process (and now has taken them all). We had a marvelous and interesting date doing things like reading each other's profiles in Please Understand Me II (I'm an INTP and she's an ENFJ). We're at near opposite ends of the spectrum there.

It might have saved our relationship and it undoubtedly gave immediate and massive benefits to our communication. We laughed and flirted over each other's differences. She soon discovered that significant others of INTPs are the only ones that have a support group online because we can be so pragmatic and unempathetic.

59   Catherine Clifford, "Jeff Bezos: I spend my billions on space because we're destroying Earth," CNBC, July 17, 2019, https://www.cnbc.com/2019/07/17/why-jeff-bezos-spends-billions-on-space-technology.html.

60   Nick Rufford, "Elon Musk and Jeff Bezos are in a two-man space race – who will win?" South China Morning Post Magazine, December 19, 2020, https://www.scmp.com/magazines/post-magazine/long-reads/article/3114155/elon-musk-and-jeff-bezos-are-two-man-space-race.

She couldn't fathom how I was okay being alone on a Friday night occasionally as that would be total sadness for her. I began to understand how an overflow of ideas would overwhelm her because she can see all the steps while I mainly see the beginning. She had this amazing spirit of enthusiasm and joy when she got fired up.

Now, years into our relationship, understanding and appreciating each other's natural tendencies and how we're wired has been absolutely central to helping my wife Seven and I navigate our understand and romance. We enjoy flirting and laughing and communicating with our zone of genius, knowing it's so different for each of us. It enhances our intimacy, our communication, our understanding, and frankly, we would not be married today if we hadn't gone through this process years ago because we are so vastly different. It has transformed what would be frequent frustration into consistent appreciation.

Five things that will enhance your growth in your zone of genius:

1. Courage to act: make bold decisive and wise decisions around implementing and using your unique zone of genius.

2. Community to test: relationships are where ideas and potential are fleshed out.

3. Feedback and refinement: an active process of reflection accelerates your growth.

4. Awareness of need: where in the marketplace can your genius be used to maximum impact?

5. Repeat steps 1-4.

The world needs demonstration more than it needs teaching. It's your duty to make yourself great for the sake of others, to live in your unique zone of genius to help others show up fully. Embrace that about your zone of genius as a unique gift that you can offer to the world in service and impact. Yes, you can reap many great rewards through your gifts, but keep your eyes focused on service.

Overarching every activity and principle is the fundamental premise that to be great, you must serve. You must do something worthwhile with your talents. Think about the men and women we recognize as great: Gandhi, Jesus, Mother Teresa, Abraham Lincoln, Frederick Douglas, Martin Luther King, Jr., Oprah, George Washington, and countless others. All of them served.

Our gifts shine brightest and are unleashed the most powerfully when we step into service, when we commit to making the world better with our own unique abilities. When you dare to bring your best in the service of others, it pulls out your best.

Claim your genius. Pursue your zone of genius. Own it. Embody it. It is you in your truest self. This is your lifelong quest.

Want the secret success formula?

Extraordinary success = extraordinary right positions + extraordinary timing + extraordinary self-awareness + extraordinary commitment.

As the ancient Greeks said, "Know thyself."[61]

Want to go deeper into living out and exploring your zone of genius? One of my coaching programs or a one-on-one session

---

61 Pausanias; W.H.S. Jones trans., *Description of Greece, Volume I.*

with me or one of my team members might be the right next step. Shoot me a DM on Instagram, LinkedIn, or FB.

> *"The place God calls you to is the place where your deep gladness*
> *and the world's deep hunger meet."*
> —Frederick Buechner[62]

*Share your results, your progress on social media and tag me so I can see the worksheets and your zone of genius coming together. I love to see it!

(I promise I'll share it out :). My IG is @themikezeller).

---

62 Frederick Buechner, *Wishful Thinking: A Seeker's ABC* (New York: HarperOne, 1993).

bonus: genius routines and genius supplements

The best engine in the world isn't going to run well if it isn't taken care of. The best brain in the world isn't going to create brilliant ideas if you're tired all the time and have no energy. You've done all this work identifying your genius, give it the best chance to show.

Smart drugs, biohacks, and ultimate 5 a.m. routines have been around forever, we just haven't always called it that.

Sigmund Freud thought cocaine was the ultimate smart drug—it even was used as an ingredient in Coca-Cola for a number of years as an extra stimulant.[63] But today, with gurus like Dave Asprey, Dr. Josh Axe, Shawn Wells, and many others, I cannot help but recommend a few supplements and routines that have a noticeable effect on my performance every day.

Let's start with a few routines that have been vital for me. My favorite routines that set the stage for optimal performance:

---

63 "Cocaine," History, August 21, 2018, https://www.history.com/topics/crime/history-of-cocaine.

1. Do your most important activities during your peak energy hours. I schedule top priority activities (no more than three) per day during my peak energy and focus hours, which are usually 6-11 a.m. I learned that, for me, it's important to not have a massive morning two-hour workout, but instead to have a great mini routine that gets me rolling, say 30 minutes. Then I dive immediately into my most valuable—not necessarily most urgent—work.

2. Go airplane mode as often and for as long as possible. Yes, once a year your significant other will get pretty upset with you for a moment when he/she can't get ahold of you and gets excessively worried. But the rest of the time, you'll get way more done because you'll be far less distracted.

3. Invest high quality time with high quality people frequently. Create highly curated and highly valuable dinner parties, wine tastings, and masterminds. The caliber of your tribe determines your altitude. How high you soar is going to be a direct reflection of your inner circle. Choose wisely.

4. Fuel yourself properly with high energy, nutrient-dense foods and drinks. Avoid fried foods like the plague as they drop your mental functioning like a rock. I love my matcha tea, my acai bowls, clean grass-fed/organic meats, wild-caught fish, organic greens and berries, plus a good dose of healthy fats. When I eat clean, my mind is clean and I'm confident you'll feel the same.

5. Keep your body in peak state. As my friend Michael Gelb, the author of *How to Think Like Leonardo da Vinci* (excellent book BTW) notes, Da Vinci himself was very adamant

about keeping himself in peak physical shape: he believed it had a direct correlation and impact on all the other areas of his life.[64] I notice that if I work out in the second half of the day, I have a second wave of mental clarity, focus and energy after my workout. When I don't keep to my four times per week workout rhythm, my brain power slumps along with my confidence and focus.

6.   Create an optimal 15-30 minute morning routine. For me, it involves about 10 minutes of exercise and stretching to wake my body up, plus a glass of spring water, splashing my face with cold water. I take a brisk walk while declaring my affirmations in the morning as I walk outside (grounding). The affirmations serve to declare who I am and the vision I'm pursuing, while a short read of a passage in the Bible or other spiritual text also serves to keep me anchored to my divine purpose to do good in the world. I also wake up consistently every day (95% of the time), weekends included at roughly the same window, between 5:15-6:30 a.m. This enables my body to get into predictable rhythms. Then I take my Genius Consciousness supplement with a glass of water most weekdays to get myself locked in. Directly afterward I make my healthy, fat-loaded matcha tea and dive into my most important work for the day.

7.   Create a wind-down evening routine. I avoid stimulants and caffeine after 3:30 p.m. and rarely have a drink or eat less than two and a half hours before going to sleep. I turn my phone on airplane mode as does my wife, and we don't

---

64   Michael J. Gelb, *How to Think like Leonardi da Vinci: Seven Steps to Genius Every Day* (New York: Dell, 2000).

allow a television or working in the bedroom. As my wife and I are winding down, we typically will put on our blue-light glasses to filter light from TVs, computers, and our household.

Let's talk about supplements for a moment because they are so vital and powerful for keeping my energy and stamina up. I take a blend of different products from different companies because each product has its own unique strength. I recommend starting with these, but continually experimenting and testing out different products because different supplements have different effects on different people.

1. Genius Brands, particularly Genius Consciousness and Genius Mindfulness. All their stuff is terrific. I feel a noticeable lift in focus and energy after taking the Genius Consciousness especially and it tastes great. Here's their website: focus products at https://thegeniusbrand.com/. Use the code: MIKEZ for 15% off. I'd recommend Genius Consciousness, Mindfulness, and Immunity Shield though everything they make is great.

2. Organifi, hands down the best tasting green juice you'll ever find. So stinking good. They have travel packs and canisters as well. Akalinity has a direct impact on your natural energy and the health of your cells and this superfood loaded green drink doesn't taste like your hippy grandmother's yucky health concoction. Reach out to Josh at Organifi at this link! https://www.organifishop.com/?rfsn=5173876.13f753&utm_source=affiliate&utm_medium=book.

3. Bulletproof's Unfair Advantage, Neuro Master, and Smart Mode. Most anything Bulletproof makes is pretty terrific frankly. But Unfair Advantages gives your brain valuable food for your mitochondria in a very digestible form which helps with mental sharpness and stimulation.

4. Anything that enhances your gut: a lot of brain functioning and mental health is directly linked to gut health. For example, if you have a lot of mental fog, you likely have a candida problem in your gut. Get your gut cleaned up and your brain will function a lot better and your genius will be able to shine through. One of my favorites is Complete Biotic by Healus Health.

5. Matcha. I love Ujido matcha. Best flavor, highest quality from 180-year-old matcha growing region. One of nature's most antioxidant rich foods, matcha helps tremendously with focus and a steady caffeine drip. https://ujido.com/

6. Acai, especially by Sambazon. High antioxidant, natural energy, great tasting. Personally, I feel great having an Acai bowl or Acai smoothie nearly every day.

7. Red light therapy devices. They promote healing and cellular rejuvenation, which is anti-aging as well. When you're in pain, it's hard to be the genius you are.

8. Swanwick blue light glasses. Blue light signals to your brain that it's daytime. So when you are winding down for the night and you're watching TV or you don't have nighttime mode on your smartphone, you're receiving a lot of blue light. Plus, most normal household lighting emits a lot of

blue light. Therefore your body is getting a lot of signals. https://www.swanwicksleep.com/pages/aa-mike-zeller-vip-discount-swannies-landing-page

acknowledgements

To my devoted and brilliant wife, for your inerrant support and belief in me. This wouldn't have happened without you.

To the team at Book Launchers, for their tireless dedication and terrific support in helping bring this project to life.

To my loyal and hardworking team, for their time, energy, and insights. Krystelle Lorraine, (who also served as editor for this book), Erin King, Ashley Preciado, Goldyn, Cintia, Marcia, and Ravi, you are each appreciated.

To my wonderful parents, for always believing and supporting me.

To Jeff Goins and Karen Anderson, for your mentorship and guidance in the book writing journey. You both have been invaluable in your guidance.

To Rajesh Shetty, for challenging me to write my first book. Your belief in me fueled this journey. You have touched thousands of lives by believing in and shifting people's destinies the way you do.

To all my clients, friends and supporters for being my occasional guinea pig. It's truly a pleasure unleashing your genius.

To the occasional hater, thank you for the fuel to my fire.

books to read

Ballantyne, Craig. T*he Perfect Week Formula: Bild Your Business Around Your Life, Not your Life Around Your Business*. Denver, CO: Early to Rise Publishing, 2019.

Eyal, Nir. *Indistractable*: *How to Control Your Attention and Choose Your Life*. Dallas: BenBella Books, 2019.

Ferriss, Timothy. *The 4-Hour Work Week: Escape 9-5, Live Anywhere, and Join the New Rich*. New York: Harmony, 2009.

Gelb, Michael J. *How to Think Like Leonardo da Vinci: Seven Steps to Genius Every Day*. New York: Dell, 2000.

Hendricks, Gay. *The Big Leap: Conquer Your Hidden Fear and Take Life to the Next Level*. New York: HarperOne, 2010.

Katie, Byron. *The Work of Byron Katie*. Byron Katie International, 2018.

Koch, Richard. *The 80/20 Principle: The Secret to Achieving More with Less*. New York: Currency, 1999.

Maxwell, John. *Failing Forward*: *Turning Mistakes into Stepping Stones for Success*. Nashville, TN: Thomas Nelson Publishers, 2007.

Newport, Cal. *Deep Work: Rules for Focused Success in a Distracted World.* New York: Grand Central Publishing, 2016.

Pressfield, Steven. *The War of Art: Break Through the Blocks and Win Your Inner Creative Battles.* London: Black Irish Entertainment, 2002.

Robbins, Tony. *Awaken the Giant Within: How to Take Immediate Control of Your Mental, Emotional, Physical and Financial Destiny!* New York: Simon & Schuster, 1992.

Wade, Cleo. *Heart Talk: Poetic Wisdom for a Better Life.* New York: Atria Books, 2018.

Wattles, Wallace D. *The Science of Being Great.* CreateSpace Independent Publishing Platform, 2014; originally 1910.

citations:

1750 January, Poor Richard Improved: Being An Almanack and Ephemeris of the Motions of the Sun and Moon for the Year of Our Lord 1750, (Poor Richard's Almanac), Benjamin Franklin, Month: January, Column: 2, Philadelphia, Pennsylvania.

The paradox seems to be, as Socrates demonstrated long ago, that the truly free individual is free only to the extent of his own self-mastery. While those who will not govern themselves are condemned to find masters to govern over them.

Pressfield, Steven. The War of Art . Black Irish Entertainment LLC. Kindle Edition.

Musk/Bezos Space race:

https://www.cnbc.com/2019/07/17/why-jeff-bezos-spends-billions-on-space-technology.html

https://www.scmp.com/magazines/post-magazine/long-reads/article/3114155/elon-musk-and-jeff-bezos-are-two-man-space-race the genius within

CPSIA information can be obtained
at www.ICGtesting.com
Printed in the USA
LVHW012329041121
702405LV00005B/9